William Taylor Adams

The Dorcas club

Our girls afloat

William Taylor Adams

The Dorcas club
Our girls afloat

ISBN/EAN: 9783337110635

Printed in Europe, USA, Canada, Australia, Japan

Cover: Foto ©Andreas Hilbeck / pixelio.de

More available books at **www.hansebooks.com**

THE DORCAS CLUB;

OR,

OUR GIRLS AFLOAT.

BY

OLIVER OPTIC,

AUTHOR OF "YOUNG AMERICA ABROAD," "THE ARMY AND NAVY SERIES,"
"THE WOODVILLE STORIES," "THE STARRY FLAG SERIES," "THE
BOAT CLUB STORIES,", "THE LAKE SHORE SERIES,"
"THE UPWARD AND ONWARD SERIES,"
ETC., ETC.

WITH THIRTEEN ILLUSTRATIONS.

BOSTON:
LEE AND SHEPARD, PUBLISHERS.
NEW YORK:
LEE, SHEPARD AND DILLINGHAM.

Electrotyped by C C. Morse & Son, Haverhill, Mass.

TO

MISS EDITH H. STEPHENS,

OF RAHWAY, N. J.

whose honored father, Henry L. Stephens, the artist, I have so often been indebted for making things plainer with his pencil than I could with my pen, in many of my stories,

This Book is Affectionately Dedicated.

The Yacht Club Series.

4

PREFACE.

THE DORCAS CLUB is the fifth volume of the YACHT CLUB SERIES, and like its fellows in the same box, is an independent story, having its own hero, and, in this instance, several heroines, with no necessary connection with any other volume of the series, though some of the characters whose acquaintance the reader has already made are again introduced. The Dorcas Society, as the name would indicate, was an association of young ladies, banded together for benevolent purposes, which did a great deal of good in a humble and quiet way. The members of this Society formed the Dorcas Club, to engage in the healthy and agreeable exercise of rowing. Not many years ago the skilful use of an oar would have been considered an unfeminine accomplishment; but happily the fashions change in matters of custom as well as garments, and now even prim maidens of uncertain age are not startled when they see young ladies at the oar. It is a pleasant and health-giving exercise for girls, and the author hopes to encourage its use.

Like the other stories of the series, the interest does not depend entirely upon the aquatic experience of the young ladies and their friends. Prince Willingood, who is the proper hero of the volume, is a young man of high aims and noble purposes who always tries to do right, though he does " strike out a course independent of his guardian,"—in this case a wicked and miserly uncle, whom it was a sin to obey, and a virtue to resist. The young reader who cherishes the same high aims and noble purposes, will become a good man or a good woman, though never called upon to act a part in events so exciting as those in the career of the hero.

TOWERHOUSE,

October 21, 1874.

CONTENTS.

7

CHAPTER VII.

CHAPTER VIII.

CHAPTER IX.

CHAPTER X.

CHAPTER XI.

CHAPTER XII.

CHAPTER XIII.

CHAPTER XIV.

CHAPTER XV.

CHAPTER XVI.

CHAPTER XVII.

CHAPTER XVIII.

THE DORCAS CLUB:

OR,

OUR GIRLS AFLOAT.

CHAPTER I.

PRIVATE AND CONFIDENTIAL.

"WHAT'S the matter, Minnie Darling? You look so pale!" said Eva Doane, the secretary, as the young lady, president of "The Dorcas Society," entered the drawing-room of Captain Patterdale's elegant mansion, where the meeting for that week was held.

"I don't know; I haven't felt very well for a month," replied the president, languidly, as she seated herself on the sofa. "I should not have come to the meeting this afternoon, if I had not felt that I must."

11

"I heard you were not well," added Nellie Patterdale, taking Minnie's white hand. "Is it the slow fever that prevails so much just now?"

"No; I have no fever; I am simply tired out, and have lost my appetite. The doctor says I don't take exercise enough."

"Well, why don't you take more?" asked Eva.

"I can't. How stupid it is to walk, for instance, when you have nowhere to go, or to do anything just for the sake of exercise!" replied Minnie, rather pettishly, as though she had tried and failed in experiments of this kind. "As soon as the warm weather comes, when we can play croquet, and stay out doors, I shall be well enough. Even then I shall envy the boys with their Yacht Club; they have such exciting and health-giving sports."

"Why can't we have something of the kind?" suggested Ruth Hapgood, the vice-president.

"What, sail boats?" exclaimed Eva.

"No, not exactly sail them, but row them."

"There isn't much fun or excitement in merely paddling about in the water," added Minnie.

"We may have a boat club, as the lords of creation have a yacht club. Why not?" said Nellie Patterdale.

"Wouldn't it be splendid!" added Mollie Longimore, one of the prettiest and sweetest of the young ladies in the room, though any one skilled in judging of feminine habiliments would have observed that she was not so richly dressed as her companions, and that she wore no costly jewelry.

By this time the attention of all the young ladies, varying in age from fourteen to twenty, was engaged in the new and exciting topic. They were mostly pupils of the high school in the city, and had formed the association for benevolent purposes. One day a poor Irish girl, who was struggling against many obstacles to obtain an education, was missed from her accustomed place in school. One of the scholars gave the information that the poor girl's mother had been burned out the night before, and nearly all the clothing of her three children had been destroyed. The master suggested that his pupils should do something for the family, in this emergency, by bringing some of their cast-off clothing for the sufferers. In a few hours more garments were supplied than the poor woman had ever possessed in all her lifetime. The girls seemed to be inspired by this deed of charity, which resulted in the formation of the DORCAS SOCIETY. It met one afternoon of each week, and the girls — many of them the daughters of the richest citizens of the place — made garments, and collected cast-off clothing, which they distributed to the poor, without distinction of sect, nation, or color. When money was needed, they raised it by carrying subscription papers to the wealthy.

Everybody who knew anything about the matter, declared that the Dorcas Society did a great deal of good, not only to the poor, but to its members, for charity is "twice blessed." In the cutting and making of garments, they were cheerfully assisted by their mothers and their maiden aunts, and being deeply interested in their employment, they made great proficiency in the arts of sewing and dress-making. Doubtless some of the wealthier ones obtained a knowledge of what they would not have been required to learn at home.

As it was a sewing society, and as the meetings were held in the afternoon, the boys of the school were very sorry to find that they could take no part in the good work; for the mothers of the girls insisted, for obvious reasons, that the young men should not be admitted to the society.

The young "lords of creation" wished to contribute money, if nothing more, to the enterprise; but even this aid was resolutely declined. Yet the attendance of one boy was requested at each meeting, by the society, who was graciously permitted to run of errands for the members, to purchase thread and needles, deliver bundles, or even, if not otherwise employed, to hold a skein of thread or yarn for winding. The mothers and maiden aunts were fully assured that there was no "flirting" in the society, which now consisted of twenty-five members.

"We could form a boat club as well as the boys," said Nellie Patterdale.

"And buy a boat," added Ruth Hapgood, "so that we could have it all to ourselves."

"How much would it cost?" asked Mollie Longimore, whose enthusiasm seemed to be suddenly checked.

" That would depend upon the size and finish of it, I suppose," replied Nellie. " My father has always said that rowing was a good exercise for girls; and he has seen young ladies row as well or better than any boys."

" Mercury," said Minnie, calling to Prince Willingood, who was the errand boy of the afternoon; and whoever held the office, he was always addressed by the name of the messenger of the gods, as, being the messenger of the goddesses, it was quite appropriate that he should be.

"Miss President," replied Prince, a good-looking fellow of seventeen, though not very well dressed.

The young man bowed low, as he stood before the chief officer of the association. His eye twinkled, and it was evident that he was just a little inclined to burlesque the forms of the society.

" Do you know anything about row-boats, Mercury?" inquired the president.

" Do I know anything about row-boats, Minnie, darling?" he replied.

" My name is Minnie Darling," said the chief officer, blushing deeply; and the girls began to

titter, as girls sometimes will, though not often on such solemn occasions as the present.

"I beg your pardon, Miss President; but I said Minnie, darling," added Prince, bowing low again.

"You will oblige me by putting your words a little more closely together, for you speak my name as you would read it if some blundering writer had put a comma between the Christian and surname."

"Pardon me; I will try to do better. *Minnie* darling — how is that?"

Though he made no pause between the two words, he emphasized the first so that the effect was the same as before.

"That will not do, sir!" exclaimed the president, sharply. "I shall punish you for contempt of court—"

"Pardon me; I have no contempt of court; for I think courting must be one of the nicest things in the world, though I don't know anything about in myself.

"I shall banish you from the Dorcas Society forever."

"Don't do that!" pleaded Prince, dropping

2

upon his knees, and extending his arms, as one might do in a play.

"As the president of this association, I will not permit such language," said Minnie Darling, severely.

"I will never do it again! I solemnly promise, I vow on the honor of a knight —"

"Silence, sir!"

"I am dumb."

"Shall this culprit be banished from our presence, Sisters of Dorcas?" continued the president, turning to the young ladies, whose mirth did not permit them to work. "Those in favor of it will say, 'Ay.'"

Not one voted.

"Those opposed will say — *exercitationibusque.*"

"*Exercitationibusque*, exclaimed several who studied Latin, and knew the word.

"By the grace of these sisters of Dorcas you are saved from banishment, Mercury; but, like General Jackson, I will take the responsibility, and drive you from this Eden, if you ever address me by any other than my official title."

"I never will, Min — Miss President — thanks for your clemency," answered Prince, bowing low again.

"I asked you, Mercury, if you knew anything about row-boats? I repeat the question."

"I do, Miss President."

"What do you know?"

"That they are used mostly in the water, Miss President."

"Indeed, Mercury!"

"They are not of much use where there is no water, Miss President."

"I see that you understand the whole subject. How much do row-boats cost?"

"From two dollars and fifty cents up to a thousand dollars, Miss President."

"That is very definite."

"Row-boats are very definite, and include everything from a calked sugar-box up to the launch of a ship-of-the-line, Miss President."

"Do you know of a light boat, in which young ladies might practise the art of rowing, Mercury?"

"I do."

"Is it for sale?"

"Alas! I know not."

"Could you ascertain?"

"I could."

"Go and do so."

"I fly on the wings of — J. Prince Willingood."

"Where is the boat, Mercury?"

"In the shop of Don John, the renowned boat-builder, otherwise Ramsey & Son, who built it with his own skilful hands during the winter which has just passed away."

"If for sale, ascertain the price, and whether it is suitable for young ladies."

"I am gone, Miss President;" and in another instant he was gone.

Prince Willingood hastened to the shop of Don John, the builder of the Sea Foam, Maud, Alice, and other celebrated yachts of the fleet. The young builder was hard at work painting a beautiful four-oar race-boat which he had just completed.

"How you was, Don John?" said Prince.

"First rate; how are you, Prince?"

"Salubrious. What are you going to do with that boat, Don John?" said the messenger of the goddesses, proceeding to business.

"That depends. Work was slack with me this last winter, and I built her more for the fun of it, and to see what I could do in this line, than for any other reason."

"Well, she is as handsome as the prettiest girl in the High School. But what are you going to do with her?"

"Sell her, I suppose, if anybody wants her."

"Then she is for sale?"

"She is, though I don't care any great about selling her. I have an idea in my head, though I may sell her."

"What's that?"

"I think I won't say anything about it now," laughed Don John.

"What's the price of her?"

"Two hundred dollars."

"Lowest price?"

"The very lowest. I will keep her for my idea rather than let her go for less."

"Is she fit for girls — for young ladies — you know!"

"For young ladies!" exclaimed Don John.

"That's what I said."

"But why do you ask such a question?"

"That's my idea, and I think I won't say any thing about it," replied Prince, demurely.

"She is just the thing for young ladies. She is very light and very strong."

" Right ; that's all ; good by, Don John ; " and
Prince turned on his heel and left the shop,
each of the young men wondering what the
other's idea was.

Mercury returned to the elegant mansion of
Captain Patterdale, and was in the presence of
the goddesses again.

" Miss President."

" Mercury."

" The row-boat is for sale."

" The price ? "

" Two hundred dollars."

" Is it suitable for young ladies ? "

" Most suitable, Miss President, for the renowned boat-builder a sures me she is very light
and very strong."

" How large is she, Mercury ? "

" I have not her length ; but she must be
thirty-five or forty feet long.   She pulls four
oars, and has room in the stern-sheets for two
at least, besides the one who holds the tiller-
ropes."

" It is well, Mercury.   Did you say aught to
the boat-builder that the Sisters of Dorcas sent
you ? "

"I said nought to him that the goddesses had made me their winged messenger, Miss President."

"You were wise and discreet. Now, good Mercury, carry that bundle to Mrs. McFinnigan, in the rear of Miller's store."

Prince departed upon the errand, and the members discussed with enthusiasm the purchase of the new boat in the shop of Don John. If twenty of them contributed ten dollars apiece, the boat could be bought at once. Poor Mollie Longimore did not say a word, and all her enthusiasm had suddenly subsided. Her father was not a millionaire, like Mr. Montague, nor a *half-millionaire*, like Captain Patterdale. His salary as the cashier of one of the banks was not large, and there had been much sickness in the family during the winter. All the children but herself had had the scarlet fever, and the doctor's bills and other expenses had been very large. She knew that her father had been much troubled about money matters, and she could not think of asking him for ten dollars to pay her share of the cost of the boat. Only the daughters of the rich men ought to expect to pay so much for such a luxury.

"We will call it the Dorcas Club," said Nellie Patterdale. "I like that name ever so much."

"So do I. That's splendid! I was going to suggest the Benevolent Boat Club," added Ruth; "but I like the old name better."

"Will the boat club and the sewing society be the same thing?" asked Mollie Longimore, with a troubled expression.

"Yes; have it the same thing," suggested Eva.

"Very well; change the name from 'society' to 'club,'" added Minnie. "Then we shall be an association for rowing and doing good to the poor."

"But we can't all engage in the boating part of the society's business," said Mollie.

"Why not?" asked Nellie, with no little astonishment.

"We are not all of us daughters of the nabobs of the city," replied Mollie, with a blush; for though she had courage enough to acknowledge the fact, it was no more than human for her to feel the distinction between the rich and the poor of society.

Indeed, it is generally the poor who feel it more than the rich.

"What has that to do with it?" asked Nellie, with a merry laugh.

"Some of us cannot afford to pay ten dollars towards the boat," said Mollie.

"We don't ask anybody to do so," added Minnie. "The purchase of the boat shall be by voluntary contribution. Certainly we shall not compel any one to pay anything."

"But those who do not pay anything will not feel like taking places in the boat," argued Mollie.

"But they must be made to feel like it," persisted Nellie, warmly. "It is no virtue on the part of any member that her father happens to be rich; and I am sure the Dorcas Society has always been as democratic as anything could be. I don't think any one of us ever thought whether a girl's father was rich or poor. Perhaps our fathers and mothers will not approve of our getting the boat."

"O, I know they will!" exclaimed Eva.

"We can ascertain before the next meeting," said Minnie.

"But Mollie has almost frightened me out of the idea of having a boat," continued Nellie, seriously. "I wouldn't have anything like an aristocracy in the club, or any feeling that one is better or richer than another. If we have a boat, she must be as much for one as for another. I wish some one would make us a present of the boat, so as to save us from this difficulty."

"Perhaps some one would, if people knew that we wanted a boat," suggested Ruth.

"We don't care to beg, or hint our wishes," added Minnie. "But it can be managed in some way. Do you suppose girls can keep a secret?"

"I know they can," laughed Eva. "I am more afraid of Mercury than I am of the girls."

"Miss President, I will never open my mouth, except to eat, outside of the lodge," protested Prince, who had returned.

"Lodge!" exclaimed the girls.

"If you are going to have a secret society, it will be a lodge," added the messenger.

"But we only want to keep the secret from each other. We don't want it to be known who contributes for the boat," explained Minnie.

"I can manage that nicely," said Nellie, going to the book-case in the room and taking therefrom a package of plain white envelopes, and giving them out, one to each member.

" What's that for?" asked Minnie.

" I will tell you," answered Nellie, seating herself again. "Each girl shall give the envelope to her father, explaining to him that we desire to purchase the boat without any of our members knowing who pays for it. She shall tell her father that no one must contribute a dollar unless he feels able to do so, and no one is to know whether he gives anything or not ; and he must be pledged not to tell of it himself. Whatever he is willing to contribute, he must put into the envelope, seal it up, and give it to his daughter, who shall hand it to the treasurer at the next meeting."

"I beg your pardon, Miss President ; but may I be permitted to offer a suggestion?" interposed Prince, who was quite as much interested in the plan as the young ladies.

"Certainly ; go on, Mercury," replied Minnie.

" Any girl can see whether the envelope contains a bill or not by holding it up to the light. Besides, all the girls won't tell the story in the same way ; and if any one forgets part of the explanation, the plan would fail. Joe Guilford has a printing press and plenty of type. He publishes the High School Amateur, you know, and does job-work besides. Suppose you write a circular, explaining the whole plan, print it, and put it into the envelope, asking the father to return the circular, with his money folded into it, in the envelope."

" Very good, indeed, Mercury!" replied Minnie; and the plan was adopted.

Nellie proceeded to write the circular, which was read and amended till it was adopted by vote. Prince was appointed to procure the printing of it. Three days later, the work was done, the copies enclosed in white envelopes, and given to the members.

The document was headed " Private and confidential," and Joe Guilford was not allowed even to keep a copy in his printing office. It was very clearly written, and appealed to the fathers to whom it was addressed to keep the secret for the good of all concerned. Those who did not favor the enterprise, and those who were unable or unwilling to give to the object, had the assurance that no one but themselves would know how much they contributed, or if they contributed at all, if they concealed the fact themselves, as they were requested to do.

Mollie Longimore received her envelope, with the other members, but she took it with some embarrassment.

"I don't feel just right about it, Minnie." she said. "Must I give it to my father?"

"There is nothing to compel you to do so," replied the president.

"My father is not able to give even a dollar; but he is proud, and he would feel obliged to do so, if I gave him the circular," added Mollie, blushing.

"Do as you think best, and I will take the responsibility, Mollie; only return the envelope at the next meeting, sealed like the others.

And Mollie decided that she would not even tempt her troubled father to contribute a single dollar to the boat. As she walked towards home, Prince Willingood overtook her.

CHAPTER II.

DINNER FOR ONE.

MOLLIE LONGIMORE was a good girl,
And if she knew that she was pretty,
she did not seem to know it. She lived in the
same street with Prince Willingood, and so it
happened that they often walked to and from
school together. It is not certain that they did
not sometimes walk together by the connivance of
Prince, though never by that of Mollie. For
this and some other reasons they were better
acquainted and more intimate with each other
than the most of their schoolmates.

Whether Mollie knew that she was pretty or
not, Prince had a decided opinion in favor of
the affirmative of this proposition; and this may
be one reason why they so often chanced to get
home from school at about the same time. Probably the young man had no very definite ideas

of love, in relation to the young lady, and had not yet made up his mind that he would die for Mollie, or even live for her; but he had a very high respect, and a very deep regard, for her.

"I suppose you have your envelope, Mollie?" said he, placing himself by her side, though at a bashful distance from her.

"Yes, I have it; but I am not going to give it to my father," replied she, decidedly.

"Why not?"

"I don't think it would be right to do so; and Minnie told me to do as I thought best. We have had some one sick in the family all winter, and father feels very poor."

"What are you going to do with the circular?" asked Prince.

"I shall return it at the meeting next Tuesday. I wish you would keep it for me till that time, Prince. I don't like to carry it home, for fear mother or father might see it. The children are always poking over my books and papers."

"I will keep it, and give it to you when you go to the meeting, for I am not Mercury next time, you know," replied Prince, as he took the envelope and placed it in one of his books.

"Thank you, Prince. I wouldn't have father see it for anything, for I am almost sure he would feel obliged to give something if he read the circular. He has pride enough for a man who is worth a hundred thousand dollars. Mother told me the other day that I must not ask him for any new dress this spring, because he is so terribly worried about money matters. But don't you tell anybody what I say, for all the world, Prince."

"Certainly not, Mollie."

"I wouldn't have said anything, but I have felt so badly about this circular ever since the plan was mentioned. I think I must withdraw from the Dorcas Society, for I ought not even to pay the dollar a year for my membership. Father has grown so pale and thin, worrying about the bills he cannot pay, that I am afraid he will be sick. Your uncle knows all about his affairs, and I suppose you do."

"My uncle!" repeated Prince, and his lips seemed to be involuntarily compressed· as he uttered the words. "He don't tell me about his business; but I think your father would be less miserable if he had some other man for his principal creditor."

"I never heard father say anything against your uncle."

"Your father is not one of the sort to do so."

"He is very patient and uncomplaining, but he suffers terribly."

At this point of the conversation, they reached the house of the cashier, and Mollie parted from her friend. Prince crossed the street, and opened the broken-down gate of a dilapidated dwelling. It looked like the home of poverty; but it was not. It was the smallest and meanest house on the street. Prince entered it at the street door, and passed into the front apartment, which was the sitting-room. Its ragged carpet, its painted chairs, scarred by long use, its broken rocking-chair, its cheap, rude secretary, the dented, smoking stove, were in keeping with the exterior of the house, and everything within and without indicated the meanness of the owner and occupant, Mr. Fox Bushwell, the uncle and guardian of the young man.

3

Prince tossed his books upon a three-legged table and passed out into the kitchen. It was half past two in the afternoon, and, like all other school-boys he was hungry. He was a growing boy of seventeen, and he was blessed with an appetite. Mr. Fox Bushwell did not so regard that appetite; to him it was a curse. Even Mrs. Pining, the melancholy housekeeper of the establishment, did not view it with favor, for it certainly increased the amount, though not the variety, of her culinary toils.

The dinner table standing against the wall, with one leaf raised, was waiting the late-comer from school. Her employer insisted upon having his meal at twelve o'clock, and Mrs. Pining groaned at the necessity of keeping Prince's dinner for him till the middle of the afternoon, as she expressed it; but as she never bestowed any extra labor on the hungry boy, he was the principal sufferer under the arrangement. The housekeeper placed the dinner on the table, and Prince stood in the middle of the room looking at the woman and at the food. He did not say anything for some time, but it was plain enough to Mrs. Pining that thought and feeling were

boiling in his mind and heart. Not that he was
a grumbler or an unreasonable young man; not
that he was given to "turning up his nose at
his victuals," for Prince was easily satisfied, and
entirely reasonable in his desires.

We confess that we have some doubts about
recording the scenes which transpired that afternoon in the kitchen and sitting-room of Fox
Bushwell's house, lest we should again be charged
with picturing a hero who rebels against his guardian, and therefore commits forgery and theft. A
boy who is bad enough to insist upon his own
clear right to decent food, when it is paid for out
of his own inheritance,— even, when driven to
desparation, to "strike out for his rights,"—
ought to be wicked enough to forge a note or steal
his friend's money. Of course boys have no rights
which a cruel and selfish guardian is bound to
respect. Of course boys are not capable of
judging whether they are misused or not; and
those who are well treated are sure to imitate
the example of those who are ill treated, if they
"strike for their rights." Even a bright boy
does not know the difference between right and
wrong. If he is well clothed, lodged, and fed,

he will so confuse and confound things as to imagine that he is deprived of the simple comforts of life!

Truly it is an awful responsibility which one assumes in telling the story of a boy, who under any possible circumstances, rebels against his guardian; and before we do so, we must solemnly appeal to all our boy-readers not to confound their own situation with that of the hero. If you dine upon roast beef, roast turkey, chicken pie, and similar luxuries every day in the week, do not consider yourself starved, and commit forgery — we beg of you, boys, don't do it. If you are decently and comfortably clothed, do not imagine that you are naked, and break into a bank. If you have a nice room at home, with a hair mattress to sleep upon, do not allow yourself to believe that you have to sleep on the hay in the barn, and pick somebody's pocket. If you have kind parents, or even maiden aunts, who love you, watch over you, and care for you in sickness and in health, though they faithfully rebuke your faults, do not imagine that you are tyranized over by cruel guardians, and get up a riot in the High School.

Of course boys from the age of twelve to twenty are utterly incapable of making distinctions, and must believe, in their own cases, that they are treated with the utmost severity, if their mothers tell them not to stay out after midnight. They can not tell the difference between their own happy lot and that of the boy who is kicked and cuffed, starved and ill treated in any manner, in the story, even if the writer of it uses his utmost ingenuity to make out as bad a case as possible for his hero. Of course the brighter the boy who lives out his real life on Murray Hill, the more likely he is to imagine himself the victim of a cruel tyrant. We hope the boys will all heed this solemn warning: do not strike for liberty until you are reasonably sure that you are a slave, or in prison, or are abused and down-trodden. Feeling confident that not a single one of our readers— after this admonition— will commit forgery because Prince Willingood was ill treated, we will go on with the story.

Mrs. Pining had put the dinner on the table, and the young man stood looking at it. Even the housekeeper saw that he was dissatisfied, and that he had the manner of one who intended mischief. It ought to be said that Prince had been a patient sufferer, and up to this time had made no trouble in the house. However he had felt aggrieved at the diet provided for him, he had hardly ever uttered a complaint.

The dinner set before him consisted of salt fish, potatoes, and hard brown bread. The drawn butter provided for the fish was very strong of warm water, and very strong of butter — not on account of the quantity of butter in it, but on account of the inherent strength of the butter itself. The potatoes, originally boiled, had latterly been baked till they were of the color and consistency of sole leather. Now, if this had been an accidental or occasional dinner, on a washing, house-cleaning, or other day of domestic casualities, I am sure that Prince would not have felt justified in turning up his nose at the fare set before him.

For our part, we cordially approve a "Cape Cod turkey," or salt fish dinner, even as often as once a week; but we insist upon the boiled beets, egg sauce, and pork scraps, which are as much its constituent elements as the fish itself.

Yet we could not stand it four times a week any more than Prince Willingood could. The staple articles of Fox Bushwell's bill of fare were salt fish and baked beans, varied with fresh fish — when Prince caught it himself. Once in a while the proprietor of the tumble-down house bought some corned beef, or "salt horse," at the ship chandler's, when it was too poor for sailors' use.

On this occasion Prince was unusually hungry, even for a school-boy. He never carried a luncheon, as most of his school-mates did, because there was nothing in the house to carry but brown bread; and his pride would not permit him to eat that in the presence of his school-mates, who took sandwitches, pie, cake, and doughnuts from their tin boxes. If his friends — and he had plenty of them — had known how it was with him, they would have insisted upon his partaking of their lunches.

That morning the oak-leaf tea had been particularly bad, even worse than the crust-coffee which the housekeeper sometimes made, and the herring had been so abominably strong and salt that he had gone to school as hungry as when he got up. At half past two in the afternoon his appetite had not diminished.

Prince was hungry enough to eat salt fish and strong butter; and probably he would have done so if he had not been considering the situation, and come to the conclusion that it was not his duty to submit to semi-starvation. He had made up his mind that he could not stand it any longer, even if the flesh was willing. He had no chance to earn any money, with which to improve his diet, or he would have done so. More than this, he was laboring under the belief that his uncle's treatment of him was a personal outrage — for this young man of seventeen was heir of over twenty thousand dollars, left him by his father, which yielded an income of at least twelve hundred a year. He had been an only child, and his parents had both died when he was quite young. They had lived in another part of the state; and though the boy's mother was Fox Bushwell's sister, neither she nor her husband seemed to have fathomed his meanness, for Mr. Willingood had made him the executor of his will, the trustee of his property, and the guardian of the child. A more unfit person could not possibly have been selected for either of these charges.

In justice to Prince's father, it should be said that Fox Bushwell had been growing meaner, more sordid, and more dishonest every day for the last dozen years, or since the death of his wife, who was a good woman, and exercised a salutary influence over him. For a couple of years after Prince was brought to the house of his uncle, the child had the kindly care of Mrs. Bushwell; but after her death he had really been alone in the world, till he made friends for himself outside of his cold and comfortless home. By the terms of his father's will he was to receive the best education the town and High Schools could afford; and this was doubtless the only reason why he was permitted to attend school up to the age of seventeen.

Prince looked at the dinner on the table, and rebelled against it. Perhaps it were better to eat salt fish for dinner for the fourth time that week than to go hungry; and if that had been the alternative, he would have eaten it. As it was, he would not.

" Have you anything else for my dinner, Mrs.

Pining ? " Prince began, as gently as he could.

" Lud a massy ! What a world of trouble we live in ! Ain't that enough for you ? " demanded the amazed housekeeper.

" I'm tired of salt fish, especially when the potatoes are all burned up, and the gravy is nothing but water," replied Prince.

" What on airth are we comin' to ? "

" Coming to dinner, I hope. No more salt fish for me — at least not more than once a week."

" This is a world of sin and sorrow," groaned the widow Pining. " We are all dyin', perishin' mortals, and can't eat salt fish ! "

" I can't eat any more of it," said Prince, as he took a butcher-knife from the tray, and passed out into the back room.

" What on airth's got into the boy?" moaned Mrs. Pining. " Is he goin' to kill hisself ? "

She followed the desperate young man. But Prince had not the remotest idea of committing suicide. He was too sensible a fellow to do anything of the kind. Probably he would not have thought of refusing to eat the salt fish, if he had not known of something better to do.

Late in the fall of the year before, Fox Bushwell had killed a hog, which he had kept in defiance of the public sentiment of this locality, and of the public health. He had sold all the best part of it, except the ham, which hung in the back room, smoked and ready for use. Why he had kept it he could not have told if he had been pressed for an answer. Certainly he had not meant to eat it himself, or to permit the other members of his family to do so; at least he had not allowed any such extravagance so far, and it was contrary to his nature to do it in the future.

Prince jumped upon a wash-bench, and took the ham from its roost on the nail. He laid it upon the bench, and felt of the edge of the knife. Doubtless his mouth watered as he thought of making his dinner from such a savory dish as fried ham. He had no remembrance of ever having tasted such a luxury at home, though he had several times cooked and eaten it on board the yachts, when he had practiced the culinary art under the instruction of Morris Hollinghead, the most celebrated cook in the fleet.

"What on airth are you goin' to do, Prince Willingood?" cried Mrs. Pining, amazed and horrified at the actions of the young man.

"I'm going to have some dinner," replied he, as coolly as he could speak, at the same time cutting off a slice of the ham.

"But, stop! World of sin and sorrer! What will your uncle say?"

"He can say anything he pleases. I'm going to have some dinner for once in my life, if I have to fight for it;" and Prince cut off another of the small slices.

"Heavens and airth! Mr. Bushwell will kill you, and kill me, too, if I don't stop this shameful waste."

"Don't you meddle. I do it myself; and I don't ask you even to look on. If you interfere, I shall fight — that's all."

"Lud sakes alive! I'm a poor creeter, in a dyin', perishing world!"

"That's so," added Prince; and he continued to cut off the small slices till he thought he had enough; and most people would have thought he was getting up a dinner for four.

Then he proceeded to trim off the slices till

they were clean and nice, as he used to prepare them on board of the yachts.

"It's wicked, Prince, in this sufferin', dyin' world, to waste all that good bacon. What do you cut all that off for?" asked the housekeeper.

"That's the way to fix it."

"No, 'tain't. You waste more'n half on't."

"I can't help it. That dirty, black outside isn't fit to eat."

"In all my born days, I never seed nobody so diffikilt. What's the world comin' to?"

"I don't know what it's coming to. I don't know that I care."

"What will your uncle say?"

"You know what he will say, and so do I; but I'm ready to face the music," added Prince, as he threw the slices into a spider that hung in the back room.

Taking an armful of wood and the cooking utensil, he returned to the kitchen. Starting up the fire, he prepared for still more active operations, watched all the time by the housekeeper. In a few moments the ham was hissing and sizzling in the spider, sending forth a rich odor, such as had not gladdened the interior of Fox Bushwell's house for many a year.

"We are all goin' to perdition!" sighed the widow Pining.

"If we are, I'm going on a full stomach," replied Prince, as he turned the ham, which caused it to redouble its music.

"You will be the ruin of us all, Prince. This dyin', sufferin' world is no place for such folks as you be. Your appetite will be the death of you."

"I'm afraid it will, if I don't do something to satisfy it."

Prince wanted to go to the closet and get some cold potatoes to fry with the ham, for he knew there must be some there for the fish-hash the next morning, which as surely followed the salt fish dinner as the rising follows the setting sun; but he was afraid, if he left his dinner, the housekeeper would carry it off. However, to prevent such a catastrophe, he bore the spider to the closet with him, and there sliced into it three or four good-sized potatoes.

"Lud sakes," groaned Mrs. Pining; "there'll be nothing for breakfast in the house, if you use up all them potaters."

"'Sufficient unto the day is the evil thereof," replied Prince, as he dished up the ham, and proceeded to cook the potatoes.

In a few moments they were done, and the hungry young man sat down at the table, with the savory dinner before him. The thought of the consequences of his rash deed did not seem to diminish his appetite, and he ate like one who had not tasted food for twenty-four hours, which was almost literally the case with him. The widow Pining was too much excited to sit down, and she stood by the table, her face the very picture of horror and dismay, while Prince devoured slice after slice of the ham, and half after half of the potatoes. Doubtless he ate all he could; but he was not quite able to "punish" all he had cooked.

"I feel better," said he, rising from the table. "I will finish what there is left in the morning."

"I shouldn't think you'd be able to go. Sufferin' and dyin' world! To think what a lot of that nice bacon you've wasted! I know your uncle was goin' to sell it," added the housekeeper. "Well, it's a wicked world we live in!

There ain't no such thing as gratitude in't. I didn't think you'd do sech a thing as steal that bacon, and waste sech a lot on't too'"

"I saved my bacon; that's the whole of it, Mrs. Pining."

At that moment the front door opened, and the step of Fox Bushwell was heard and recognized.

"Now you'll ketch it, Prince Willingood!" said the housekeeper, in a low and impressive tone.

"I'm ready," answered the young man, as he strained up his nerves to meet the onslaught.

Fox Bushwell came into the kitchen at once. He came snuffing with his peaked nose, as though he smelt something. Perhaps he "smelt a rat," as well as fried ham.

"What's this smell all over the house?" he demanded, in his whining, high treble voice.

At that moment his eyes rested on the remnants of Prince's feast on the table, and his thin, hatchety face contracted into an agglomeration of frowns, which were intended to annihilate the woe-begone housekeeper, to whom his glance was directed.

CHAPTER III.

THE BATTLE FOUGHT AND WON.

MR. FOX BUSHWELL was fifty-five years old, but he was thin, gray, and wrinkled enough to be seventy-five. From the force of habit rather than in deference to the decencies of life, he shaved his furrowed face twice a week, leaving the wiry white beard under his chin and beneath his jaws. His hair, of the same color, was generally very long, because it cost money to cut it, since the removal to distant parts of a cousin, who used to do the job gratuitously, with the sheep-shears. We do not like to say it, but this man had formerly been a preacher. He had picked up education enough to enable him to obtain a license. He had been regularly settled in a small place; but a pastorate of two years had convinced his people that the Rev. Fox Bushwell had missed his calling; that his piety

4

was a pretence, and his life a mockery of his preaching.

For a few years more he supplied vacant pulpits as occasion offered ; but then his father died, and left him ten thousand dollars, a like sum passing to his only sister, Prince's mother. He already owned the small house in which he lived, and the large lot of land on which it stood. This territory he sold in small parcels, as the growth of the city increased the value of the lots. Events led him to become a money-lender. He would sell a lot, and advance money to the purchaser to build a house upon it, taking a mortgage on the whole for security. He was a hard man, and scrupled not to take advantage of the needy, extorting extravagant interest, and taking possession of mortgaged property upon the slightest failure to comply wtih the conditions. It cost him next to nothing to live, for he believed that money spent upon the body was wasted.

The patrimony of his nephew enlarged his capital upon which to speculate on the wants of the needy; and, though he made it pay eight, ten, or twelve per cent., he returned only legal

interest on his accounts. As a mean man becomes
meaner as he grows older, Fox Bushwell, when
he was fifty, was a miser, a skinflint, an extor-
tionist, and a thief. This was simply describing
him as he was, and as we knew him — for he
is not a fancy sketch. He had sold some of the
houses in his street two or three times, for non-
payment of interest or principal. Of course he
was generally hated and despised by those who
had any dealings with him.

At the death of his wife, he had procured the
services of Mrs. Pining as housekeeper. She
was not much more than half-witted, but she
had loaned a few hundred dollars to her employer, — her dowry from her late husband's
estate, — the interest of which was her only
income, for Fox Bushwell paid her no wages.
The poor woman was as credulous as she was
simple, and had been kept in her place by
mingled hope and fear. She had somehow obtained the notion that the money-lender intended
to marry her. Doubtless something to this effect
had been said by him; at any rate, he was careful to keep alive the delusion. This was her
hope; and she feared if she left her situation

her tyrant would cheat her out of her little fortune, thus leaving her a begger in "this sufferin', dyin' world." This woman, with her hopes and fears, had had the principal care of Prince Willingood from his childhood.

The property of the young man was charged five dollars a week for his board; and this sum more than paid the whole living expenses of the family. Fox Bushwell purchased his clothing, which was of the plainest and homeliest quality. Altogether the young man's expenses were not more than four hundred a year, leaving a surplus of twice that amount from his income. Not till just before his introduction to the reader had Prince considered his financial relations to his uncle. In fact he knew nothing about them till by diligent inquiry he obtained the information, with the assistance of friends, from the records of the Probate Court. As has been stated before, he had come to the conclusion that he was entitled to fare better than he did, and even to have an occasional dollar for pocket money, as other boys of his age had.

Fox Bushwell stood in the kitchen, gazing at the remnants of his ward's dinner. The odor of

fried ham was as much unknown in that house
as though its inmates had been true followers
of Mohammed, the prophet of Islam. The skinflint was amazed and horrified, and turned his
gaze to Mrs. Pining.

"What does this mean?" he demanded, in
the husky tones he might have used if a mur-
der had been committed in his house.

"'Tain't none of my doin's," pleaded the
housekeeper. "Look here, Mr. Bushwell;" and
she led the way to the back room, where she
pointed with horror, and in significant silence,
at the leg of ham lying on the wash-bench, just
as Prince had left it, with the rind and parings
at its side.

"Who cut that ham?" growled the miser.

"Sufferin', dyin' world knows I hadn't nothin'
to do with it," groaned Mrs. Pining.

"Who did it, then?"

The widow Pining pointed silently in the
direction of the kitchen, whither Fox Bushwell
instantly returned.

"Did you cut that ham, Prince?" he demanded,
with a scowl which only a mortal sin ought to
have conjured upon a human face.

"I did," replied Prince, squarely.

"You did?"

Prince nodded.

"What made you do it?" continued the guardian, confounded by the coolness and self-possession of the young man.

"I wanted some dinner."

"Dinner! Didn't you have your dinner of salt fish and potatoes, as I did?"

"Sufferin', dyin' world! He had just the same as the rest on us," added Mrs. Pining. "I kept his dinner for him, as I allers does; and it was good strong victuals for anybody, and enough on't."

"It was strong of bad butter, I grant," replied Prince. "I am so tired of salt fish that I can't eat any more of it. I have tried to eat it; but I can't stand it any longer."

"You can't?" gasped Fox Bushwell.

"No, sir, I cannot. It is salt fish for breakfast and salt fish for dinner more than half the time; and when it isn't salt fish, it is smoked herring or baked beans. The poorest common laborer in the city lives better than I do, and better than you do, uncle Fox."

" Don't you have enough to eat"

" I don't complain so much of the quantity as I do of the quality. It don't matter how much there is on the table, when it is so poor that I can't eat it."

" Indeed! Has it come to this?" said the uncle, severely.

" It has come to this. My dinner to-day was salt fish, with potatoes cooked to a chip, with drawn butter mostly water, but so strong at that I could not bear the smell, much less the taste, of it," continued Prince, calmly. " For breakfast I had a thin smoked herring, so salt and strong I could not eat it. I had hardly tasted anything since dinner yesterday, when I came into the house this afternoon."

" You are getting dainty," sneered Fox Bushwell.

" I don't think I am. But whether I am or not, I shall stand this thing no longer.'

" You won't?"

" No, sir."

" We'll see."

" Both of us will see."

There was something in the tone and manner

of the young man which made an impression on the miser.

"And you cut that ham which I have been saving all winter?" he added.

"I did."

"Is that ham yours?"

"While it is in the house where I board I claim an interest in it."

"You've got to eat what's set before you; and you haven't any right to touch anything else. That ham belongs to me, and when you took it you stole it," said Fox Bushwell, warmly and sternly.

"I should like to be taken up for stealing it, I should like to tell the justice all about it, and read to him our bill of fare for any week in the year," replied Prince. "We might as well have this matter understood now. You receive five dollars a week for my board

"Who told you that?" demanded the guardian, evidently startled by the statement.

"I got it from good authority."

"I can charge anything I please, and the judge can allow it or not, just a he likes."

"Five dollars a week is the price you said you should charge. I can prove this.'

' Well, it's cheap for taking care of a boy, and looking after his washing and mending, his manners and his morals.

" Never mind the manners or the morals. It don't cost you much to attend to them. For the sum I pay, I am entitled to as good board as mechanics and laborers have at the same price. If you will pay my board in a sailor's boarding-house, I will be satisfied."

" I shall do nothing of the sort," protested Fox Bushwell. " I give you enough to eat, and that which is good enough."

" I don't think so ; and something must be done about it."

" You want to run away — do you?"

" No, sir, I do not. I have no intention of running away."

Fox Bushwell wished he would run away, and never return; it would simplify his accounts as trustee of the boy's property.

" You live as well as I do; and what's good enough for me is good enough for you."

" I don't think so."

" I don't care what you think. But what I have in the house hereafter, I shall keep under lock and key."

" My father left twenty thousand dollars to me, in your care. By this time, taking out all my expense, it ought to be at least thirty thousand, at simple interest, six per cent. My income to-day ought to be eighteen hundred dollars; and I have to live, week in and week out, year in and year out, on salt fish, smoked herring, baked beans, brown bread, and strong butter."

" The living is good enough for me, and so it is for you," muttered the uncle, amazed to find that his ward knew something about his own finances.

" We differ; and as the income of my property is eighteen hundred dollars a year, I insist on something better, whether I have it in this house, or some other. More than this, being seventeen years old, I want a little money to spend myself.'

" You do!" exclaimed Fox Bushwell, aghast at such unheard-of impudence.

" I do. As the matter stands now, I can't buy a sheet of paper, a pencil, or a book."

" I have bought all those things for you."

" You refused to buy four books for me the other day, when I asked for them.'

" You didn't need them."

" I wanted them, and I think I am able to own those, and many more."

" I can't countenance no such extravagance. It isn't necessary for you to own books of history."

" We differ, and I may as well come to the point. I am going to live decently — I mean as well as laborers and sailors live. If my breakfast to-morrow morning should be salt fish, or herring, or baked beans, I shall get my meal at the eating-house, and have it charged to you as my guardian."

" I won't pay it!" protested Fox Bushwell.

" Perhaps you will in the end. At any rate, Hoxley says he will take his chances of collecting the bill."

" Have you been telling Hoxley that you havn't lived well enough at home ? " demanded the guardian, angrily.

" Sufferin', dyin' world ! " ejaculated Mrs. Pining, moved deeply by this new aspect of the case.

" It was not necessary to tell him or anybody else that we live worse than the Irish laborers.

Everybody knows it. In the second place, I want an allowance of ten dollars a month, for the present, to purchase books and other things that I need."

"Ten dollars a month! Are you crazy, Prince?" cried Fox Bushwell. "Ten dollars a month to a boy of your age! I didn't think you could be impudent enough to ask for more than twenty-five cents a month, at the outside."

"Ten dollars I ask for, and ten dollars I shall have, besides decent board."

"The boy's insane!"

"Sufferin', dyin' world!" groaned the widow.

"It's no use for you and me to argue the point; we can never agree."

"Never! You won't get any ten dollars a month out of me, nor ten dollars a year. That's the way to spoil boys."

"And the board, as the allowance, is denied? Shall I be fed as well as common sailors?"

"I'm not going to have any extravagance in my house."

"Very well, uncle Fox; it is my next move," replied Prince, rising from his chair.

"What are you going to do?" asked the guardian, evidently much troubled by the conduct of the boy.

"I don't know that it is necessary for me to tell you; but I'm going to do something immediately."

"Humph! What can you do? I'm your guardian."

"I know you are; but you may not always be."

"What!"

"I don't believe that in this free country a boy who has, or ought to have, an income of eighteen hundred dollars a year, can be legally starved, or half starved, and deprived of the common comforts of life, uncle Fox! I don't believe it. I don't believe that I can even be deprived of the luxury of books. I'm rich enough to board at the best hotel in the city; but I ask only plain food."

Fox Bushwell drew a long breath, and perhaps his thin face was a shade paler than usual, though that was hardly possible.

"I don't know what you mean to do," whined he, alarmed at the prospect of any possible action on the part of the boy or his friends.

"I haven't talked about this matter much out of the house; my pride would not let me do that. I don't want to make any trouble now; but I won't stand this state of things much longer. No, sir, I will not."

"Things have gone on just as they always did; and I didn't know there was any trouble."

"Very well, uncle; if you are disposed to do the right thing by me, the matter need go no farther," added Prince, gently.

"But ten dollars a month to spend!" gasped the guardian.

"For books and other things I need. I don't smoke, chew, drink rum, or play cards; and not a cent of the money will be improperly used."

"It would spoil you."

"I don't think so. I am old enough to know how to use a small sum of money."

"If you don't drink or smoke, it's because you never had any money to pay for cigars and rum."

"We won't argue the matter on such a basis. If you have nothing else to say, I shall take the next step."

"What do you mean?" demanded Fox Bushwell, anxiously.

Prince considered a moment, and then took from his pocket a paper, which he handed to his guardian.

"What's this?" said the uncle.

"It will speak for itself."

Fox Bushwell put on his spectacles, and proceeded to read the document. As he did so, his lip quivered and his frame trembled. Probably the paper was not in legal form, but it was a petition to the judge of the probate court, setting forth that the petitioner's guardian — Fox Bushwell — had become evidently unsuitable to discharge the duties of the position, requesting his removal, and the appointment of some proper person in his place. The petitioner then proceeded to specify in detail that he was deprived of the ordinary comforts of life; that he was compelled to subsist almost wholly upon salt fish, baked beans, and smoked herrings; that he was clothed with the coarsest garments, much inferior to those worn by persons of his income, and he was denied the privilege of purchasing any books or newspapers needed for the proper cultivation of his mind, while the property in the hands of his guardian yielded, or ought to yield, an income of eighteen hundred dollars a year.

"You villain! What do you mean to do with this paper?" gasped the guardian, trembling in every fibre of his frame.

"I intend to present it to the court," replied Prince, quietly.

"You do?"

"I do, sir. I don't mean to strike for liberty and decent living on my own hook. I am willing to leave the whole matter to the judge. I am willing to submit to him, and to the guardian he appoints. If he says it is all right as it is, I have nothing more to say."

"Do you mean to give this to the judge?"

"Of course I do, if I can't have fair play without doing so."

Fox Bushwell was furious for the moment, and tearing the paper into a hundred pieces, he threw them into the stove.

"We'll see if you will," gasped he.

"That was only a copy of the petition," added Prince, mildly.

"WE'LL SEE IF YOU WILL," GASPED HE. Page 64.

The guardian cooled off again, realizing that
he was utterly helpless against the strong-minded
young man, who seemed to act with a conscious-
ness that boys have rights.

"Don't do anything rash, Prince," said he.
"I will think over what you have said."

"You may think over it till next Monday
morning. The court meets in the afternoon;
and my paper goes in then, if at all," replied
Prince.

Fox Bushwell went into the front room, where
he paced the apartment for hours, thinking over
the situation. Prince spent the evening in the
kitchen, studying his lessons. When he got up,
rather later than usual, the next morning, the
grateful odor of fried ham saluted his senses,
and he was almost willing to believe that he
had won the battle. For his dinner that day,
he was rather surprised to see some fried mutton
set before him. It was cheap and poor meat, it
is true; but it was a luxury to him.

On Monday morning his uncle gave him a
ten-dollar bill; but he did it with groanings and
reproaches. Prince took the bill, and enclosed
it in the white envelope which Mollie had in-

5

trusted to his keeping, and carefully sealed it. At school that day, she handed it to the treasurer, without suspecting that there was anything but the circular in it. She did not even ask Prince why he had sealed it; she did not think enough about it to do so.

"But the envelopes are to be handed in at the meeting to-morrow," said Nellie Patterdale, the treasurer.

"Please to take it now, for I may not be at the meeting," replied Mollie.

"O, very well, if you desire it; but I hope you will be there."

"I shall try to be present."

But she was not.

Great events occurred on that particular Monday, and on Tuesday Mollie did not even think of the meeting. Poor girl! she had enough else to think of.

In the middle of the afternoon Mr. Longimore, the cashier, called upon Fox Bushwell. Even the hard-visaged miser saw that he was in the deepest distress.

"Mr. Bushwell, I am in trouble, and I must raise some money before to-morrow morning, or be ruined," said the cashier, with emotion.

"Ruined! What's the matter?" asked the money-lender, willing, as usual, to profit by whatever misfortune had overtaken his neighbor.

"I am in the most abject misery to which a man was ever reduced," groaned Mr. Longimore.

"Eh? Been using the money of the bank?" added the miser, looking over the top of his glasses.

"I have overdrawn my account. I have not stolen anything. I have not altered the books, but have charged myself every dollar I have taken. I must have five hundred and twenty dollars to balance my account, or I shall lose my situation. The directors make an examination to-morrow."

"That's bad."

"You have the money in the bank, and you will lend it to me?"

"Without security?"

"Take my house, my furniture, everything, if I can save my honor," pleaded Mr. Longimore.

"I've got all the mortgage on the house I want; and I've got to go away now."

"I will pay you any interest you want. Only

lend it to me for a few days, and I will appeal to my brother in Portland for help; he will save me from ruin, I know."

"I can't stop now to talk about it. I will see you this evening," said Fox Bushwell, rising from his chair.

"I will come here — "

"Well, no, I guess not," interposed the money-lender. "My boy will be in the house then; and he is always sure to know what's going on."

"Come to the bank, then; I will be there," added Mr. Longimore, earnestly.

"I will be there about seven o'clock."

The cashier withdrew; and at the hour appointed, Fox Bushwell entered the bank.

CHAPTER IV.

THE FIRE AT FOX BUSHWELL'S HOUSE.

MR. LONGIMORE was a rather tall and spare man. Though but five and forty years old, he was quite gray, and his expression at this time was very sad and troubled. He had been struggling to support his family on a small salary, and it was apparent to him now, if never before, that he had signally failed. Doubtless he had his faults and his weaknesses; but he had always been regarded by the community in which he resided as a strictly honest, high-toned, and honorable man. He stood well in the church, and well in society; and so far as the possibilities of any disgraceful conduct were concerned, he was considered as incapable of it as any clergyman in the city.

Perhaps it was a misfortune for Mr. Longi-more that his position in the bank brought him into contact with the *elite* of the city ; with the prosperous merchants, ship-builders, and the wealthy men who had retired from business. He was respected and esteemed by all, and the cashier and his family were, to some extent, drawn into social relations with the wealthy and refined class of society. Without intending to exceed his income in his expenditures, Mr. Longimore had unfortunately been led to do so, and much sickness at home had increased his debt. He had overdrawn his salary at the bank ; but then he had faithfully charged himself with every dollar he had taken, and there was no fraud, or even concealment, on his part. Mr. Longimore was a proud man, and he could not endure the thought of seeing a frown upon the brows of the directors when they examined his accounts and looked over his securites. He could not bear to be censured, even mildly, by the men with whom he was on such friendly terms. He preferred to throw himself into the power of the unscrupulous money-lender, rather than make a candid but humiliating statement to the directors, who were really his friends.

Mr. Longimore had bought the house in which

he lived of Fox Bushwell, paying five hundred dollars down, and giving a mortgage for twenty-five hundred. But the property was supposed to have increased in value, and the cashier hoped to obtain the sum he needed by a second mortgage on the house, or on his personal effects, if the money-lender would not advance him the money he wanted for a short time without security. He had often assisted the miser in the management of his affairs, had examined his bonds, mortgages, and other papers, to insure their correctness, thus saving him the expense of legal fees. He had filed all his papers for him in the nice and convenient form in which those of the bank were arranged, and he felt that he had some claim to the consideration of the hard man.

The cashier was in the bank when Fox Bushwell arrived. He had been cutting off the coupons of a package of bonds, and was tying up the bundle with red tape when his visitor came in. He looked more worried and disturbed than the money-lender had ever seen him.

"What have you got there?" asked Fox Bushwell.

"Bonds; the interest is due to-morrow, and I have cut off the coupons, in order to send them for collection," replied Mr. Longimore, rather vacantly. "Thought I would do it while I was waiting for you, for I shall be very busy to-morrow."

"How much is there in that pile?" asked the money-lender, as he seated himself at the table opposite the cashier.

"Only forty thousand dollars."

"That's a good deal of money," added Fox Bushwell as he picked up the package.

"I should think it was if it only belonged to me," replied Mr. Longimore, with a sigh. "I should be a happy man if I had only a quarter of it. I have already told you why I wish to see you, Mr. Bushwell."

"Well, you have, but I don't understand the matter very well," added the miser, still toying with the bundle of bonds. "I believe you said you wanted to raise some money."

"I must have five hundred and twenty dollars by to-morrow morning, or I am a ruined man. I did not know how badly I stood with the bank till I balanced my account this afternoon."

"I don't see how we can manage it," said Fox Bushwell. "Of course I can't lend money without security."

"I will give you a second mortgage on my house. The equity in it is worth a thousand dollars."

"I guess not," drawled the Shylock, with a sickly smile. "I don't believe it would fetch any more than the mortgage under the hammer."

"I am sure it would. I have been offered more than I gave for it."

"The place wouldn't fetch it now, and in a year or two it might be worse than it is now. I don't like to take too much on any property. I'm a poor man, and I have to keep on the safe side."

"Then I will give you a bill of sale of my household furniture, including the piano, worth in all, at least a thousand dollars," pleaded Mr. Longimore, actually trembling with emotion.

"I don't like that kind of security," replied Fox Bushwell, shaking his head.

"But I will write to my brother in Portland immediately; he is able and willing to help me out of this trouble; and I will return the money in a few days with an ample bonus. I will give you fifty dollars for the use of the sum I want one week."

"Yes; but the security? If you should die, you know. We all mean to be honest and serve the Lord as well as we know how, but any of us may die."

"The bill of sale of my furniture will cover it, and save you from any possible loss. If I should die, my wife would pay the debt out of the proceeds of my life insurance," continued Mr. Longimore, desperately, and with the agony which an honest, honorable man feels in the face of probable disgrace.

"All these things are very uncertain. I don't like to lend money without knowing whether it is coming back to me or not. I'm a poor man, and the loss of five hundred and twenty dollars would ruin me. I'm older than you are, and I don't want to be a beggar at my time of life. I'll let you have the money you want for one week, and won't ask you any more than the fifty dollars you offer for the use of it, though it is cheap, considering the risk I run."

"You will run no risk, Mr. Bushwell."

"Certainly I do run a great risk — too great for a poor man like me to take. It makes me shudder to think of being a beggar after I'm too old to preach or to work. I can't lend money on any such conditions; but I'll tell you what I will do."

"Well, what? Anything I can do I will do," said Mr. Longimore, catching at the hope thus held out by the money-lender, who was still holding the package of bonds in his hand.

"These are thousand dollar bonds, I suppose?" asked Fox Bushwell, craftily.

"They are."

"Give me your note for five hundred and seventy dollars, payable in one week, and I'll let you have my check for the amount you want to get you out of this difficulty."

"I will do it!" exclaimed the cashier, promptly.

"Stop a minute; I haven't got quite through. You let me take one of these bonds for security —"

"But the bonds are not mine," interposed the cashier.

"I know that as well as you do. This is

the easiest way I know of to manage the business," pursued the money-lender. "You arn't going to steal the bond, or anything of that sort. When you pay the note, I give you back the bond, and no harm done to any one. Don't you see it?"

"No, I do not, Mr. Bushwell. I would not do that on any account. I have no right to take the property of the bank for my own use."

"Haven't you taken five hundred and twenty dollars for your own use?" asked the money-lender, with a sneer.

"No bond shall go out of the bank for any such purpose. I would rather face the directors, and tell them the whole truth, than do anything of that kind."

"You are too particular for your own good, and I must believe you don't think you will be able to pay the note when it becomes due."

"I am almost sure my brother in Portland will assist me. If he will not, I can raise the money in some other way. I have a great many friends in this city."

"I don't think much of friends in money matters. If you want to let me take that bond, you shall have the money."

"I could not if I would. The directors will make an examination to-morrow morning," pleaded Mr. Longimore,

"They won't miss one bond; or, if they do, you can make it right with them somehow."

"Lie to them?" groaned the cashier, ashamed and humiliated even to discuss such a question. "Let me say, once for all, that I will not use the bonds of the bank, or anything else belonging to it, to save myself. I will lose my situation, and become a beggar to-morrow, rather than become a defaulter for a thousand dollars, or any other sum."

"It strikes me that you are a defaulter now for over five hundred dollars. But you can take your choice; it is none of my business."

"But I did hope you would help me, Mr. Bushwell. I have assisted you a good deal in taking care of your business," added the cashier reproachfully.

"I don't deny it; but if I've got to pay five hundred and twenty dollars for what you've done, I had better paid a lawyer."

"I will give you a hundred dollars for the use of the money one week," said Mr. Longimore, more desperately.

" And the security ? "

" A bill of sale on my furniture, dated ten days ahead. It will be yours, if I don't pay you by that time," added the cashier.

" It's rather risky."

" Not at all."

" The note to be for six hundred and twenty dollars ? "

" Yes."

" I wouldn't take no such risk for any other man. As you say, you have helped me a good deal about my business, and filed my papers for me. I want to help you if I can," mused Fox Bushwell, snarling up his long gray hair by combing it with his bony fingers. " I don't like to do it; but I guess I'll take the risk. Six hundred and twenty dollars, you said—didn't you ? "

" Six hundred and twenty; and I will give you the note and bill of sale to-night, if you will let me have the check."

" If I'm going to do it, I might as well do it now as any other time. It's risky business; and if I get sent to the poorhouse, you must try to do something for me," replied Fox Bushwell, laying the bundle of bonds upon the table, which the cashier was careful to pick up on the instant, and place in a tin case.

Mr. Longimore wrote the bill of sale, specifying all the principal articles, but including everything in the house, and signed it. He passed the paper to his hard creditor on the other side of the table, and proceeded to make the note. When it was done, he tossed it over to the miser, with a blank check for him to fill out. Fox Bushwell had put on his spectacles, and was carefully reading the bill of sale.

"But this document ought to have a witness to the signature," suggested the creditor.

"Very well; we can have it witnessed when we go out, replied Mr. Longimore.

"Better have the note witnessed, too. I don't want anybody to think I took advantage of you; and everything must be fair and above-board."

"I don't object. The same person can witness both papers."

Fox Bushwell filled out the blank check for five hundred and twenty dollars, on which he was to pay interest at the rate of six hundred per cent.

"That makes it all right," said Mr. Longimore, as he proceeded to gather up the other papers which belonged in the tin case, and which were kept in the bank vault.

"Just a moment before you go," interposed the money-lender. "I want to ask you about a mortgage I have, that will be due next week."

The cashier seated himself again. Fox Bushwell took from the breast pocket of his coat a package of papers, consisting of deeds, mortgages, notes, polices of insurance, and other documents. The bundle looked precisely like the package of bonds in the tin case, for they were both done up by the cashier, with the same tape and covering, the papers having been folded on the same tin. The miser asked his question, which involved a discussion of half an hour, and the church clocks were striking nine when they finished it.

"Now, if you'll let me have half a dozen blank checks, I'll go home," said Fox Bushwell, rising from his chair, with the package of private papers in his hand.

The cashier had to go to another part of the bank for the blanks. While he was gone, Fox Bushwell took the bundle of bonds from the tin case. He looked at it earnestly, and his eye lighted up with a diabolical cunning. Instead of restoring the bonds, he placed the package of private documents in the tin case.

When the cashier returned, the money lender stood by the table, with the package in his hand. Mr. Longimore looked at the contents of the tin case; he even lifted the bundle which he supposed was the bonds. He did not even suspect that it was not the bonds. Why should he? No one could have told one package from the other except by reading the label upon it, written in the large, clerkly hand of the bank officer.

"It wouldn't do for me to lose these papers," said Fox Bushwell, leering and smiling, as he placed the bundle of bonds in his breast pocket.

"I should think it was hardly safe to keep them in your house. They might be stolen, or burned," answered the cashier, rather indifferently, as he locked the vault, in which he had just placed the tin case.

"No danger; I keep them in a safe place — a good deal safer than that vault. A good many banks have been broken into one time and

another," said the money-lender. "And that
reminds me that I want to tell you where I
keep my papers, so that if anything should
happen to me, sombody would know where to
find them. I don't tell my boy, or Mrs. Pining;
I can't trust them."

"But you want those papers witnessed, Mr.
Bushwell," suggested Mr. Longimore.

"We can do that at my house. Prince shall
witness them. Your folks like him," chuckled
the usurer; "and if anything happens, they
won't believe *he* means to cheat them, if I do."

"Very well; Prince shall witness the bill of
sale and the note."

Mr. Longimore carefully secured the doors and
windows of the bank building, and then walked
to the house of Fox Bushwell. Mrs. Pining had
gone to bed, but Prince was still studying his
lesson in his comfortless chamber over the front
entry. He was called down, the cashier acknowledged his signature on both papers, and
the young man wrote his name as witness upon
each of them. He read enough of the documents to comprehend their nature, and only
regretted that the father of Mollie was obliged

by his needs to mortgage his furniture, as he understood the transaction to mean.

"Now, go to bed, Prince; and don't burn the lamp till midnight," said the money-lender.

Prince returned to his chamber, and resumed the Latin translation upon which he was engaged when called.

"Now I will show you where I keep my papers," said Fox Bushwell, when the young man had left the front room.

"Of course I don't want to know, unless you wish it," replied Mr. Longimore.

"I do wish it. I'm getting old, and may die any day. I want you to know where my papers are, so that they need not be lost or destroyed," continued the money-lender, taking the lamp, and leading the way to the cellar.

From a place near the top of the wall, over a large pile of shavings, and under one of the great cross-timbers of the frame of the house, Fox Bushwell took a stone of considerable size. It was all he could lift from such a height, and its removal from the wall left a considerable aperture. Reaching into the hole, he took out a brass kettle, which contained a quantity of papers.

"That's my safe," said Fox Bushwell, exhibiting the kettle, which he held near the lamp, on a barrel. "No thief would ever think of looking behind that stone any more than any other."

"But your house might be burned," added the cashier.

"Well, the fire wouldn't touch those papers, if it was."

"The fall of that large timber over the hole would throw down the wall. But if you are satisfied, I am."

"Of course you won't tell any one," added the miser.

"Certainly not," replied Mr. Longimore, indifferently.

Fox Bushwell put the bundle, which the cashier supposed consisted only of his creditor's private papers, into the kettle, restoring the latter to its place in the wall. Lifting the stone, he adjusted it so that it seemed to be as it had been since the house was built. He filled the chinks with small stones, and then conducted his visitor up stairs.

"If I should die, you will know just where

to look for my papers, Mr. Longimore," said the usurer, as he opened the front door.

"Suppose you should die; what am I to do with your papers?" asked the cashier. "Have you made a will?"

"No, not yet," replied the miser, with something like a shudder, for men like him cannot think of giving away their property, even when they have no further use for it.

"Such things ought not to be deferred too long, you know, Mr. Bushwell."

"I know it; and I'm going to attend to the matter right off."

"I believe Prince is your heir. At least, I never heard that you had any other near relation," added Mr. Longimore.

"Well, I haven't got much to leave, and it don't make much difference," said the usurer, to whom the subject appeared to be very disagreeable. "Good night, Mr. Longimore."

"Good night; but I advise you to set your house in order, Mr. Bushwell; not only your temporal but your spiritual house; for death comes like a thief in the night."

"I'll take care of it," said the money-lender,

partly closing the door, to hasten the departure of the no longer welcome guest.

The cashier hastened away to his home. He had it in his mind to have a very serious talk with his miserable neighbor, in regard to the things beyond this life, for it seemed dreadful to him that a man should continue to pile up riches, with no thought of the hereafter. But not much time did Mr. Longimore give to the subject on that Monday night, for his own troubles weighed heavily upon his mind. He was safe from the censure of the bank directors; but he had to pay six hundred and twenty dollars within ten days, or lose his furniture, lose even the piano with which Mollie could earn her bread by teaching music, if he should be suddenly taken away. Before he went to bed, he wrote a long letter to his brother in Portland, detailing very precisely the nature and extent of his financial embarrassment, and asking for an immediate loan, to enable him to pay his note when it became due. He enclosed the sheet in an envelope, directed it, and put a postage stamp upon it. He left it on the table, and went to bed. He had not the courage to tell

his wife what had happened; and he permitted
her to sleep on, unconscious of the heavy burden
which he was bearing. He could not sleep, for the
future seemed full of trial, even under the most
hopeful view he could take of it.

Fox Bushwell's room was the front chamber,
next to Prince's. He usually retired at nine
o'clock, to save burning the lamps; but to-night
he did not come up to his chamber as usual,
and his nephew wondered where he was. The
young man had heard the door close when the
cashier left the house, and had also heard his
"good night."

Prince wondered why his uncle did not go
to bed; and at ten o'clock he went down for a
drink of water. Doubtless he went for the
water, but certainly he also wished to ascertain
what the old man was doing. Fox Bushwell
was not in the front room, nor in the kitchen,
and Prince soon discovered that he was in the
cellar. There was nothing strange in his being
there, and the young man went to bed. Perhaps the tea he had drank for supper had been
too strong — an impossible thing a few weeks
before; perhaps the Latin he had studied in the
evening had boggled up his brains; at any rate,

he could not sleep for a while. He was sure
his uncle had not come up stairs when he heard
the clock strike twelve; but the young man did
hear him shortly after that hour. His uncle was
certainly more considerate than usual, for he
seemed to be very careful about making any
noise which might have disturbed the other
inmates of the house. He had evidently taken
off his shoes down stairs, and come up in his
"stocking feet." If the door and the bedstead
had not creaked, Prince would not have known
that his uncle had retired.

"But the nephew was tired enough to sleep
by this time; and he did sleep, but not for a
long time. He was awakened by a furious yel-
ling in front of the house. Prince leaped from
his bed, and was going to the window, when he
heard the startling cry of "Fire!""

Then he smelt smoke; then he was conscious
that there was smoke in the room where he was;
then he heard the crackling and roaring of flames;
then he heard the screams of Mrs. Pining.
Drawing on his trousers hastily, he opened the
door. The entry was full of smoke, and down
the stairway he could see the light of the flames.

He rushed into his uncle's room. The old man appeared to be still asleep.

"Fire! uncle Fox!" he shouted, almost dragging his uncle from his bed.

Then he rushed to the assistance of Mrs. Pining; but the housekeeper was already descending the stairs.

"The house is afire! Sufferin', dyin' world, the house is afire!" she screamed.

Prince helped his uncle down stairs, for he seemed to be half paralyzed, so that he could not move alone; and they got out of the house at the last moment it was possible to do so by the stairs, which were now in flames.

CHAPTER V.

AFTER THE FIRE.

THE cry of " Fire," in the middle of the night is always an appalling sound, and the fact is appalling when the flames burst from a dwelling-house, where men, women, and children may be sleeping, unconscious that the devouring element is at work so near them. The cry startled those who lived in the street where the conflagration broke out, and in a few moments a crowd had gathered near the doomed dwelling.

Prince had assisted his uncle to put on a part of his clothes, and, with the rest on his arm, had actually dragged the half paralyzed money-lender into the street, where he finished his toilet. Fox Bushwell was trembling with anguish at the loss of his house, or with some other emotion unexplained. When he had put on his coat, he felt in the pockets of it, as if to assure himself of the safety of whatever papers might be there. He seemed to be satisfied in this respect.

"O, my house, my house!" he groaned, in real or apparent anguish; but no one seemed to pity or care for him.

"Sufferin' and dyin' world!" cried Mrs. Pining. "The eend of the airth is come, and there ain't no peace for the wicked!"

Crowds of men, and even of women and children, came, hurried from their beds in the dead of the night by the startling cry, or by the glare of the flames. The engines came, but before the line of hose could be laid and the brakes manned, the roof of the house fell in, with a crash, and a cloud of sparks and cinders rose into the air. The building was nearly all gone when the first stream of water was directed upon the mass of fire. It was impossible to save a timber, or even an article of furniture, and the first water had been thrown upon the adjacent houses, that the flying firebrands might not carry destruction to them. Doubtless the fire was well managed, because it was not permitted to extend to the wooden structures around it.

In half an hour the fire had done its work with remarkable thoroughness, and nothing but a few timbers was left of Fox Bushwell's house. The engines continued to play upon the blackened embers till not a spark of fire remained among them. The crowd went back to their beds, and the engines returned to their stations. Mrs. Pining had taken refuge in the house of a neighbor, to which she had been invited, and only a few lingered around the ruins.

Among the first who had come to the fire was Mr. Longimore. His troubles banished sleep from his eyelids. He heard the cry of "Fire!" and, looking out the window, he saw the flames bursting from the side of the money-lender's house. He reached the scene of the excitement just as Prince was hurrying his uncle out of the front door. With some of the more active of the neighbors who had arrived, he attempted to remove the furniture from the front room. The old secretary and the dilapidated chairs were carried out; but then the flames drove the men from the house, and it was

not safe to enter again. The cashier thought
that the fire had broken out in or near the
heap of shavings which he had noticed in the
cellar, and he wondered if the brass kettle containing the papers of his neighbor could with-
stand the heat. When nothing more could be
done, the cashier looked for Fox Bushwell in
the crowd. He found him sitting upon the
doorsteps of a neighboring house, bewailing his
misfortune in the presence of a knot of men
and women who had gathered around him.

"I am ruined, Mr. Longimore!" exclaimed
he, recognizing the cashier by the bright light
of the fire. "My house is gone!"

"You ought to be thankful that your life was
saved," replied his debtor.

"I am thankful for that. I should have
burned to death if Prince had not waked me
up," groaned Fox Bushwell. "I was sound
asleep when it broke out. But I am ruined!
I can't afford to loose so much."

"Had no insurance?"

"None to speak of — only a thousand dollars."

"Well, that will nearly cover the loss."

"O, no. I can't build another house for less

than two thousand, and all my furniture is gone!"

The cashier did not believe the miser would suffer much loss, if he had a thousand dollars of insurance. But he was astonished to learn that his neighbor had any insurance; and cer- tainly no sane agent or company would have taken any more upon the property. Whatever risk he ran, the miser was not in the habit of paying out any money which he was not com- pelled to disburse, and had boasted that he never insured any houses that he owned.

"How did your house take fire, Mr. Bush- well?" asked the cashier.

"I haven't the least idea," replied the money- lender, blankly.

"When I looked out, the flames were break- ing out at the window in the middle of the house, near the place where we went down cellar," added Mr. Longimore.

The usurer looked at his neighbor, as the fire lighted up the thin, pale face of the latter, and said nothing for a moment.

"I didn't know where it broke out. I didn't know anything about it till Prince woke me

up," said he, with more energy than he had
before displayed.

"Can't you think how it happened to take fire?"

"I can't form any idea. I went to bed about
half past ten, and didn't hear anything till my
boy called me, and hurried me out of the
house," replied the miserable man. I am afraid
somebody set the house afire."

"Who should set it on fire?"

"I don't know. Perhaps somebody got mad
because I made them pay me what they owed;
but I can't think of anybody that would do
such a thing," whined Fox Bushwell.

"Did you go down cellar after I left you?"
inquired Mr. Longimore.

"Yes, I went down to fix the kindlings for the
fire in the morning."

"What time was that?"

"About ten o'clock, I think."

"You had a lamp, of course."

"Yes; I couldn't do anything in the dark.
I put the lamp on the barrel, just as I always
do, while I split up the kindlings."

"If anything took fire from your lamp, it
would have shown itself long before the flames
burst out."

"Certainly it would; I don't believe it got afire from my lamp. Somebody must have set the fire."

"But it came from the inside," suggested the cashier."

"I don't know whether it did or not."

"I do, for I saw the flames breaking out through that middle window on the lower floor."

Fox Bushwell and the cashier talked till all the listeners had left them and gone to their beds again, till the fire was extinguished, and the engines had left.

"Was the note I gave you burned?" asked the bank officer, in a low tone, when they were alone.

"No; that was in my pocket-book," answered the money-lender. "I only put my bonds and mortgages into the brass kettle."

What do you think has become of that brass kettle by this time?"

"O, I think that's safe."

"I don't believe it is. Even the large floor-timbers were burned off, and fell into the cellar," said Mr. Longimore, gently, as though he did not wish to destroy the hopes of the usurer.

"You don't think my papers are burned up
—do you, Mr. Longimore?" groaned Fox Bushwell.

"I'm afraid they are. You ought to have
kept them in the bank vault."

"I don't think the bank's a safe place. Robbers are always breaking into banks," muttered
the usurer.

"But we can soon see whether the papers
are burned or not. I will get a lantern, and
we will see if we can find the brass kettle."

The cashier went to his own house, and soon
returned with the lantern. They walked over
to the ruins of Fox Bushwell's house. There
was scarcely anything left of it—only a few
blackened timbers which had fallen into the
cellar. They had been drenched and soaked
with water by the engines, and great puddles,
which had not yet soaked into the earth, stood
beneath them. On the side where the brass
kettle had been concealed, the wall had fallen
over, as it had also in other places, making a
practicable causway into the cellar.

"You see now how it is," said Mr. Longimore, pointing to the fallen wall.

7

"They cheated me when they laid those stone," replied the money-lender. "They didn't half lay the wall, or it wouldn't have fallen over."

"That may be; but it wasn't a proper place to keep valuable papers," said the cashier, rather severely. "I have told you more than once that I would keep your papers in the bank vault. But it is no use to talk about it now."

"You know as well as I do that a great many folks have lost their bonds by keeping them in bank safes, when they have been broken into by robbers," whined the miser. "I never thought it was safe."

"I hope your papers are safe, but I think it is hardly possible," added the cashier, as he began to examine the ground where the wall had stood. "The brass kettle must have been carried over into the cellar when the wall went down."

Mr. Longimore, with the lantern in his hand, led the way into the cellar. He rolled over a few of the smaller stones, and presently discovered the brass kettle, bottom up, and crushed in by the rocks which had fallen upon it.

"Here it is!" exclaimed the cashier, as he drew the kettle from the rocks.

"Is there anything in it?" gasped the usurer, as though his life or death depended upon the answer.

"Nothing at all; it was upside down."

"Everything gone! I'm lost! ruined!" groaned the usurer. "I might as well die now."

"It isn't quite so bad as that," added Mr. Longimore, in soothing tones. "The mortgages must be on record, and the notes will be duplicated by the makers of them."

"I don't know about that. Even the policy on the house was burnt," said Fox Bushwell, in dismay.

"The company will pay the insurance all the same," continued Mr. Longimore, poking over the rubbish to see if he could find anything from the kettle that had escaped the flames.

Nothing combustible could have passed through that fiery furnace, and it was clear enough to the cashier that all of his neighbor's valuable papers had been consumed.

"What on earth am I going to do?" moaned the usurer.

"I don't think you will loose much. Those who owe you will give new notes, and your insurance will nearly rebuild your house. Come, I think we had better get out of the night air. Prince has gone to my house to sleep, and you can share the bed with him."

"No: I guess I won't go there. I've got an empty house down the street, and I am afraid somebody will set that afire, if I don't look out for it," replied Fox Bushwell. "If you will lend me that lantern till morning, I'll stay there.'

"But you have no bed to sleep in; the house is not furnished," protested the cashier.

"It's almost morning now; and I couldn't sleep if I went to bed, I feel so bad. I shall have to move into that house, and I want to get it ready. I must go to work on it as soon as it's daylight. I can't afford to board at a hotel."

"Come to my house to breakfast, Mr. Bushwell."

"Perhaps I will; I'll see."

Fox Bushwell took the lantern, and walked down the street towards the house from which

he had recently ejected the owner for non-pay-
ment of the mortgage note. It was like the
one which had just been burned ; but, being
newer, it was in much better condition. He
took the key from his pocket, and entered the
house ; but what he did there for the next hour
does not yet appear.

Mr. Longimore walked to his own home,
where his family were again slumbering after
the excitement caused by the fire. He sat down
in the back parlor, on the table of which lay
the letter he had written in the evening. He
began to think over the events of the night.
He tried to set up some theory of the possible
or probable origin of the fire in Fox Bushwell's
house. There were many ways that a fire might
be kindled, which could not be explained after
the premises were destroyed. The mice might
have got among the friction matches ; the lamp
rags might have ignited by spontaneous com-
bustion ; a live coal in the ash barrel might
have lighted a shaving ; and some enemy of the
usurer — perhaps the man he had driven from
the vacant house — might have thrown a lighted
match into that heap of shavings. It was possi-

ble, too, that Fox Bushwell had set the house on fire, in order to obtain the insurance, though he would not have been likely to remain in his bed, if he had done so until the flames had nearly cut off his retreat.

It was a profitless consideration, and the cashier went to sleep in the rocking-chair in which he sat, for he did not care to awaken his wife by going to bed. He slumbered only an hour, and when he awoke, it was nearly daylight. He had intended to go to the bank before breakfast, in order to do some writing which the visit of the usurer had prevented him from finishing the evening before. On his arrival, he opened the vault to obtain his books, for he desired to balance his personal account before the directors appeared; and some of them generally came early in the morning, to read the newspapers, which the porter brought at six o'clock. He punched Fox Bushwell's check for five hundred and twenty dollars, which he had received the night before, and charged the account of his hard creditor with the amount for which it was drawn. He also placed the sum to his own credit, thus balancing his personal account, which he ruled off, and felt happy that he could not be censured even by a look of displeasure. He wrote the other two entries necessary to make his own and the usurer's standing correct with the bank.

He had brought the tin case from the vault, for he had placed the check in it for the night. When he took it up to return it to the safe, whether voluntarily or involuntarily, he raised the package of bonds. As his eye glanced at the label on the bundle, he started back with an emotion of horror; his heart rose to his throat, and the blood seemed to be frozen in his veins and arteries. He staggered to the table, and dropped upon it the case, retaining the package in his hand. His gaze was fixed upon the indorsment of the bundle, in his own large and plain handwriting. His frame trembled all over, and the cold sweat stood upon his brow as he read the label, —

PRIVATE PAPERS OF FOX BUSHWELL.

The cashier sank back, exhausted by his violent emotions, into an arm-chair behind him. He groaned in the heaviness of his spirit.

The trival mortification which had menaced him had been avoided to be succeeded by shameful disgrace and utter ruin. He trembled, he wept, he uttered a despairing groan when he thought of his wife and children, who, innocent as they were, must share his disgrace and ruin to the end of their days. Gathering courage from his desperation, he sprang up, and proceeded to examine the tin case.

Perhaps the bonds were still there. Vain hope! they were not there. He opened the package of "Fox Bushwell's private papers." By some inexplicable magic they might be changed into the bonds. Alas, they were only the mortgages, the single policy, and the notes of the miserable usurer, which had thus been saved from the fire. He even searched the vault for the lost package, catching, at a straw, the faint hope that he might have put it in another place, and forgotten it. The bundle was not to be found. He had seen his soulless creditor put one package into his pocket. He had seen him holding the bonds in his hand, while he made the Shylock bargain with him. He had seen the two bundles lying on the table at the same time, and he distinctly remembered that he had put the bonds back into the case with his own hands. He had unwittingly made this awful blunder? He could not believe it.

If Fox Bushwell's private papers had been put in the tin case, the bonds had gone into the pocket of his contemptible visitor. If the wretch had made this blunder, the bonds had been placed in the brass kettle, and burned to ashes. Mr. Longimore was almost insane at the thought. For a moment he dashed wildly up and down the room, and then, as if decided what to do, he put the package of papers in his pocket, restored the tin case and the books to the vault, and locked the iron doors. Seizing his hat, he walked at a furious pace to the vacant house where Fox Bushwell had taken refuge from the chill air of the night. He kicked and pounded at the door without rousing the money-lender, who, perhaps, did not care to see him. Then, in his desperation, he thrust his naked fist through a pane of glass, heedless of the blood that followed the onslaught, with the intention of unfastening the sash, so that he could obtain admission by the window. But the crash of the glass brought Fox Bushwell to the door.

"What do you mean, Mr. Longimore, by destroying my property in—"

"Silence, man!" thundered the cashier, as he seized the quaking money-lender by the throat. "You have ruined me, after all!"

"Why, what do you mean, Mr. Longimore?" whined the usurer. "Don't hurt me. Are you crazy?"

"I am crazy! mad! beside myself! If you don't answer me, if you don't speak the truth, I'll tear you in pieces, as a lion does a goat!" roared the cashier.

"Let me alone! Don't hurt me! I'll do anything. I'll answer you. I always speak the truth."

"Where is the bundle of bonds?" shrieked Mr. Longimore, shaking his clinched fist in the pale face of the miser.

"What bonds? I don't know what you mean."

"You do, you villain! What have you done with them?"

"I haven't got any bonds, and I don't know what you mean. Don't be so savage: I'm afraid of you."

"You may well be afraid of me, if you don't give up those bonds! What have you done with them?"

"I haven't seen them. I don't understand what you are talking about," whined the trembling scoundrel. "Don't hurt me! I'm a clergyman."

"You are a knave and a villain; and if you were ten times a clergyman, I would tear you in pieces, if you don't give up the bonds," said Mr. Longimore, more mildly, but still furiously.

"I can't understand you," pleaded Fox Bushwell, livid with terror.

"Do you see that?" demanded the cashier, producing the miser's package of papers, which he gave to the other.

"Why, Mr. Longimore! these are my papers! My mortgages! my policy! my notes! I thought they were all burned. God bless you, Mr. Longimore, for saving them from the fire! I'll pray for you! I'm a clergyman; and I'll pray for you always!" cried the money-lender, with a ghastly smile on his livid face.

It seemed to be real; and, quivering with

emotion, the cashier gazed upon the wretch before him.

"You left this package in the bank, and took the bundle of bonds—forty thousand dollars in bonds!" gasped Mr. Longimore. "What have you done with them?"

"I took the bonds?" said Fox Bushwell, opening his eyes and his mouth to their widest tension.

"You did."

"I didn't mean to take them, if I did. I thought they were my private papers. You know the two bundles were just alike. You fixed them both, with the same wrapper and the same red tape," whined the usurer. "I took the bonds instead of my bundle—did I?"

"You did!" groaned the cashier.

"I didn't know it. I didn't mean to take the bonds. I'm a clergyman, and I can't tell a lie."

"What have you done with them?"

"With what?"

"With the bonds."

"I put the bundle which I thought was mine into the brass kettle. If it was the package of

bonds — I — they — were — all — burned," said
Fox Bushwell, with a shudder.

"I am lost! I am utterly ruined! O, my
wife, my children!" groaned Mr. Longimore,
beating his forehead with his hand.

Suddenly he turned and fled from the house.
Fox Bushwell watched him till he disappeared
in the distance; then he looked upon his bundle of papers, and a hardly perceptible smile
played for an instant upon his lips.

CHAPTER · VI.

OPENING THE ENVELOPES.

"PLEASE to come to order," said Miss Minnie Darling, the president of the Dorcas Society, when the hour appointed for the meeting arrived, on the Tuesday following the events narrated in the last chapters.

It was early on the morning of that day that Mr. Longimore had rushed, in an agony bordering on distraction, from the vacant house where Fox Bushwell had taken refuge. The fair members discontinued their chatter instantly, for they were deeply interested in the coming proceedings of the meeting. They ceased to talk all together, as enthusiastic girls are apt to do; indeed, they ceased to talk at all. The secretary read the minutes of the last meeting, the regular routine business was transacted, and several applications for aid were presented by members

who had learned of poor people needing clothing or other necessaries since the last week.
Certainly everything was done "decently and
in order;" but it must be acknowledged that
there was far less interest than usual in the ordinary proceedings. Doubtless the vision of a
swift-flying race-boat, propelled by fairy rowers,
was flitting through the minds of most of
them.

The last clause of the minutes of the preceding meeting was to the effect that "Donald John
Ramsay, otherwise 'Don John,' was appointed
Mercury for the next week." This was a matter
of so much importance that even a person generally so busy as the active representative of
the firm of Ramsay & Son, boat-builders, felt
that he could not decline it; but it so happened
that business was just then at a stand-still
with him, and it was a positive pleasure to spend
the afternoon in the presence of so many charm-
ing young ladies, especially as Nellie Patterdale
was a prominent member of the association. At
the time when all the routine business of the
meeting had been done, however, Don John had
not yet put in an appearance; and no such

thing as the non-arrival of the the young man
who was honored with the title of Mercury to
the goddesses had ever been known. He had
always been on hand when the members were
called to order, and, besides feeling like a fly in
a honey-pot, he regarded himself as highly com-
plimented by the appointment.

" Where is our Mercury?" asked Eva Doane.
" There is no one to send with the garments
voted at the last meeting."

" He treats us with contempt in not making
his appearance," added the president. " Did you
notify him, Miss Secretary?"

" I did, in the usual form, and requested him
to inform me if he was unable to accept the
appointment," replied Eva.

" He incurs our displeasure by slighting our
expressed wishes," continued Minnie Darling.

" I am sure something unexpected has detained
him." said Nellie Patterdale; and there was a
slight blush upon her face, as she realized, after
she had begun to speak, that she was apologiz-
ing for one whom she was supposed to regard
with more than ordinary favor. " Don John is
always at the post of duty, and always punctual,

"SILENCE, MAN!" THUNDERED THE CASHIER.   Page 106.

·

unless he is sick, or detained by circumstances absolutely beyond his own control."

"I suppose so," laughed Ruth Hapgood.

"We all know that Don John is a model young man, and we are willing to believe that the sky has fallen, or that some other equally disastrous event has prevented his attendance," said the president. "Therefore it is our presidential pleasure that he be heard before he is condemned, reproved, or reproached. We are ready to attend to the business of opening the envelopes, which I intended should be done by our Mercury, so that no mark, dot, scratch, or indentation shall enable one of our own number to identify the enclosure of her father or guardian. We must find some other person to perform this duty. Who shall it be?"

"I will go for my brother," suggested Nellie Patterdale.

"That involves a delay," replied the president.

"My cousin, Philip Jelley, from Bangor, is in the house," said Ruth Hapgood, at whose residence the meeting was held. "He arrived today noon; and when I told him we were to have

8

a meeting of over twenty young ladies this afternoon, he declared that he was a lucky fellow,
and had tumbled into the sugar bowl. When
I informed him that we allowed no gentleman
to attend our meeting, except Mercury, he
threatened to commit suicide by drowning himself in a wash-bowl."

"He is in the house — is he?" asked the
president.

"He is; and, if he has not already committed
suicide, he is available for use."

"Bring in the Jelley," added Minnie Darling. "We are all dying to know what is in
the envelopes. We appoint the Jelley Mercury,
pro tem."

Ruth soon produced the young gentleman
from Bangor, who was formally presented to the
president.

"Minnie, darling, I am delighted —" he began.

"Stop, sir!" interposed the president, with
dignity. "That is a stale joke, an unpardona-
ble offence. Whoever, of the lords of creation,
makes a pause between her first and her last
name, in addressing the president of this asso-

ciation, shall be instantly and forever banished
from our presence."

"I beg ten thousand pardons; and, under the
circumstances, if I were drowning, I would not
stop the millionth part of a second, for breath,
between your first and last name," protested
Philip Jelley. "I am ready to serve you with
my fortune, my life, and my sacred honor, and
to dispense Bangor chivalry like dew among the
rose-buds."

"It is well, Mr. Jelley. We accept your apol-
ogy and your promise to sin no more. We have
work for you to do."

"I would I were a Hercules instead of a
Mercury, then, that I might slay the Nemean
lion, demolish the Lernean hydra, overwhelm the
Erymanthian boar — "

"Stay; you will become a bore yourself if
you intend to recite the exploits of Hercules,
for we know them by heart," interposed the
president.

"Forgive me. I am dumb till my task is given
out," replied the young man, amid the general
tittering of the girls, who saw that the president was more than a match for the glib-speak-
ing gentleman from Bangor.

"Our forgiveness flows as freely as water to the truly penitent. Play the *role* of Mercury, and not of Hercules," continued Minnie. "You will open those envelopes in the basket, pass whatever bank bills they contain to the treasurer, and announce the amount taken from such enclosure. You will stand alone in the corner, as you do so, and be particular to observe the instructions I give you, Mr. Jelley."

"I will obey to the letter."

"Obey in spirit, as well as to the letter."

Nellie had placed the basket containing the envelopes in a chair in the corner of the room. In another chair was a second basket for the envelopes and circulars, when the money had been taken from them.

"You will stand alone in the corner, with your back to the audience — "

"With my back to the ladies?" gasped Mr. Jelley.

"You will obey me in letter and in spirit," the president proceeded. "You will face the corner while you open the envelopes and take the money from them. You will be sure that no young lady sees the one from which you take

a bill. You will throw each enclosure and the
circular it contains into the waste basket on
your right. Then, with the money in your hand,
and nothing else, you will right about face, and
announce the amount, which will be recorded
by the secretary. You will next step forward,
and hand the amount to the secretary. Do you
understand me, Mr. Jelley?"

"Perfectly; and I will carry out your instructions in spirit, and to the very letter, protesting
against nothing but the penalty of being compelled to turn my back to the ladies, even for
a single instant," replied Mr. Jelley, who, for a
young man of eighteen, appeared to have an
astonishing self-possession in the presence of such
a bevy of laughing girls, whom it is ten times
as difficult to face as it is twice as many full-
grown women.

"By our presidential command you do so; and
therefore we pardon any seeming discourtesy in
the act."

"But I am the only sufferer," protested Mr.
Jelley.

"Then suffer in silence, or decline the charge
we have imposed upon you, and we will seek a
more willing Mercury.

"None could be found in this humdrum age, or even in the classic days of yore."

"You have the caduceus; proceed with the business, or vacate the premises."

"I am as dumb as a mute, but as active as a French dancing-master," answered Mr. Jelley, as he hopped into the part of the room where the baskets were awaiting him. Facing into the corner, he took up one of the white envelopes, broke it open, and took therefrom the printed circular. From this he removed a greenback, and having deposited the now useless papers in the waste-basket, he faced about with military precision. The members of the Dorcas Society were breathless with interest and excitement, and perhaps the graceful military salute which the messenger made was entirely lost upon them.

"Miss President."

"Mercury."

"I have the honor to — "

"Announce the denomination of the bill, without any flourishes whatever," interrupted the president, impatiently. "You will say, 'One dollar,' 'Five dollars,' or 'Ten dollars;' 'only

this, and nothing more;' not another word, or
no longer shall you be Mercury."

"Imperial Juno, I—"

"The amount!"

"Ten dollars."

"It is well. Advance, and give the bill to
the treasurer."

Mr. Jelley obeyed, marched with military precision to the chair of Nellie Patterdale, wheeled
about and returned to the corner.

"Five dollars," said he, when he had, in the
same manner as before, possessed himself of the
monetary contents of another envelope.

This small amount produced a slight reaction
in the minds of the members, from hope to fear
that the aggregate would be insufficient for the
purchase of the boat.

"Ten dollars," said Mercury, next.

Hope revived again.

"Ten dollars," was the succeeding announcement.

By this time Mr. Jelley seemed to have fully
learned his lesson, and he did not add a single
word beyond the requirement of the president.
When he had opened the next envelope, he

faced about, and, having made the military salute, he stood like a statue, and as dumb as one. The president and the members waited impatiently to know the amount of the bill in his hand; but he continued to maintain his obstinate silence.

"Announce the denomination of the bill," said Minnie Darling.

Mr. Jelley bowed, but opened not his lips.

"What ails you?"

Mercury wrote upon a slip of paper with a pencil, "May I speak?" which he presented to the president with the utmost deference.

"I command you to speak."

"I beg pardon; but I cannot announce the amount in the last envelope without exceeding my instructions," replied the messenger. "You commanded me to say, 'One dollar,' 'Five dollars,' or 'Ten dollars;' 'only this, and nothing more.' As this bill in my hand is neither of these, and is something more, I dare not speak."

"You go by the letter, and not by the spirit, Mercury. The letter killeth, but the spirit giveth life."

"I think it will in this case, Miss President,"
added the messenger.

"We will amplify our instructions so far that
you may give the denomination of the bill, whatever it may be; but only this and nothing
more."

"Fifty dollars," said Mr. Jelley, bowing, and
advancing to the treasurer.

This announcement was followed by a general
titter and a general clapping of hands; but it
was succeeded by two of only five dollars each,
which depressed the tone somewhat. Then came
several tens and one twenty. For the twentieth
time the messenger faced about, and saluted the
president. He did not immediately speak, and
seemed to be laboring under the temptation to
make a speech, which, however, he was able to
resist, though he made his announcement with
extraordinary flourish.

"One hundred dollars!"

"Goody!" "Goody!" "Splendid!" "Capital!" "Elegant!" "Magnificent!" cried the
members from all parts of the room, as Mr.
Jelley advanced to deposit the large bill in the
hand of the treasurer. "We have more than

enough now!" "It's a sure thing!" "What glorious times we *shall* have!"

The next announcement was of another fifty, and the last was a twenty.

"The business is completed, Mercury, and we present our thanks for the very acceptable manner in which you have discharged your duty," said the president.

"Must I go now?" asked the gentleman from Bangor. "I have opened twenty-five envelopes, and I estimate that I have spent twenty-five minutes with my back turned to the goddesses of this assembly, which was, therefore, all lost time to me. I implore you, Miss President, compensate me for this sacrifice by permitting me to remain for a space of time equivalent to that of which I have been cheated by my implicit obedience to your presidential commands."

"Not because you deserve any other reward than our thanks, which have been presented to you, but because we may have further need of you, are you permitted to remain."

"Thanks, Miss President!" And the messenger seated himself at the side of Ruth Hapgood.

While this conversation was going on, Eva Doane was adding the amounts recorded, and Nellie Patterdale was counting the money.

" Well, Miss Secretary, what is the result?" asked Minnie Darling.

" Let us see if my figures agree with Nellie's count, first," said Eva, as she and the treasurer compared notes.

"Stop a moment," interposed the president. " I have forgotten one thing. — Mercury!"

" Miss President," replied Mr. Jelley, springing to his feet, and saluting as before; and it was supposed he was, or had been, a member of some military company.

" If any one or more of the envelopes you opened contained *no* money, you are solemnly enjoined not to mention the fact," added Minnie.

" But, Miss President, every one of them did contain money," responded Mercury.

" Now, Mercury, you have spoiled the whole!" exclaimed the president, with an expression of deep chagrin. " Why did you say anything?"

" I implore your presidential pardon," said the messenger, bowing low. " You told me if one

or more of the envelopes contained *no* money, I
was not to mention the fact. As every one of
them did contain money, from five dollars to a
hundred, I respectfully and reverentially submit,
there was no fact to conceal."

"I am sorry anything was said," added Minnie.

" But it can make no difference," interposed
the secretary, " for I have recorded and numbered
twenty-five donations; and I am sure no one
can have the least idea who gave the five dollars, and who the fifties, and the hundred."

"It is all right," protested several of the
girls.

"If it were not all right, it could not be
helped," said Minnie. "You will read the
amount, Miss Secretary."

" Four hundred and fifteen dollars," replied
Eva Doane, consulting her paper.

" Four hundred and fifteen dollars!" repeated
the president.

This announcement was followed by the clapping of hands, and by all the ejaculations contained in the young ladies' vocabulary. The
amount of the contributions was unexpectedly

large; indeed, they were double the sum anticipated by the most sanguine. In the circular
the probable cost of the boat had been stated,
and a majority of the donors had evidently com-
puted, and given what appeared to be their fair
share, with some allowance for the possible failure of a portion to contribute. On the other
hand, it was evident that the one who had enclosed the hundred, and the others the twenties
and fifties, believed that a considerable number
of the members' fathers or guardians would give
nothing, and had been very generous in order
to prevent the defeat of the plan. But none of
the girls had the remotest idea who had given
these large sums. At least a dozen of their
fathers were able to give the largest amount;
and, of half that number, one was as likely to
have done it as another. It was by no means
certain, even, that the poorer parents had enclosed the five-dollar bills, since some of the
richest men in the city were the meanest and
most penurious.

It was with a feeling of real pain that Minnie Darling realized that Mollie Longimore, who
was not present at this meeting, had not done

as she had said she intended to do Her father must have given at least five dollars, for every envelope contained money, and this was the smallest amount in any. Perhaps something in her manner had induced Mollie to change her purpose, and the poor, harassed cashier had felt obliged to contribute. Minnie was sorry she had not spoken more decidedly to her friend, or that she had not given the envelope to her own father, with an explanation, for he was more able to give a thousand dollars than Mollie's father was one. But she was determined to see Mollie, when she could speak to her alone, and have the money returned. She felt that it was a shame and an outrage for one so burdened with trials and troubles as she had heard Mr. Longimore was, to be asked, or even permitted, to give five or ten dollars for such a luxury as a row-boat.

"We can buy Don John's boat at once," said Nellie Patterdale. "If she is ready, we can take our first lesson in rowing to-morrow."

"Who shall be our instructor?" asked Eva.

"O that I might be the happy fellow!" exclaimed Mercury, *pro tem.*

"Do you understand rowing?" inquired Minnie.

"Alas, no! I don't know an oar from a bottle of Day & Martin's blacking!" groaned the messenger.

"Commodore Montague, Don John, Ned Patterdale, and a dozen more, know all about it," added Ruth. "But we have members enough to fill the boat five times."

"We can have another boat!" exclaimed Eva, her eyes flashing at this rapturous thought.

"Two boats!" shouted some of the girls, wild with delight at the prospect which was thus presented to them,

"Certainly; we can purchase a second boat immediately," added Nellie. "But even two are not enough to enable us all to row at the same time."

"Our girls afloat! Why was I born that my lot should be cast in Bangor, instead of here!" sighed Mr. Jelley.

But the girls gave little heed to the rhapsodist from up the river. They were excited, and they all talked to together, discussing plans for the future. It was all confusion; but it was sweet confusion, for there is nothing in the world more delightful than five and twenty, or even half a dozen, girls full of life and animation, with from two to a dozen ringing out their silvery tones at the same instant, as though life were all too short to enable them to speak one at a time. The president rapped with a pencil on the table to bring order out of this confusion, so as to propose a method by which all might fairly use the boats. At this moment Don John was announced.

The arrival of the boat-builder created a decided sensation. He was the man of boats, and he could tell them whether or not the new boat could be used the next afternoon, or even that very evening, for the weather was warm and pleasant for early May. He could tell them when they could have the second boat; and he could tell them who was best qualified to instruct them in the art of rowing. Don John was doubly welcome, therefore, and no one even thought of hearing his excuses for not presenting himself in season to discharge his duties as messenger.

But there was something about Don John

which seemed to embarrass them. Instead of wearing his best suit, as he was in the habit of doing when he went into the presence of young ladies, he wore his working clothes. More than this, his garments were covered with mud and dirt; his face was begrimed with grease and tar, and streaked with lines where the perspiration had run down from his brow. Besides, his expression was full of trouble.

"I hope you will excuse me for being late, Miss President," he began, with much emotion and excitement. "I was so busy that I did not think of this meeting till the minute I started to come to it. Of course you have heard the news?"

"What news?" asked Minnie.

"About Mr. Longimore."

"We have heard nothing."

"He has disappeared; nothing can be found of him," replied Don John.

"Mr. Longimore!" exclaimed several of the girls.

"He has not been seen since the fire last night, though it is certain he was at the bank this morning," added the boat-builder.

9

"But what has become of him?" asked Nellie.

"No one knows. The bank directors did not think much of it till they ascertained about noon that a package of forty thousand dollars in bonds was missing."

"How awful!" exclaimed Eva.

"Mollie Longimore was not at school to-day," said one of the girls.

"Do they think he has run away with the money?" inquired Ruth.

"The directors are afraid he used the bonds some time ago. If he had intended to run away, they think he would not have waited till this morning. Mrs. Longimore and Mollie say he has been much troubled lately. In a word, they fear he has committed suicide."

"Poor Mollie!" sighed the president, bursting into tears.

She was not the only one who wept as the members thought of the agony poor Mollie must be suffering at that moment.

CHAPTER VII.

THE FIRST LESSON IN ROWING.

"IT is so dreadful!" exclaimed Eva Doane, wiping the tears from her eyes. "To think of Mr. Longimore doing anything wrong! It seems to me quite impossible."

"I suppose he was in debt, and the temptation was too much for him," added Ruth Hapgood.

"I do hope he has not committed suicide," continued Eva, with a shudder; "that is so awful!"

"Of course no one knows that he has done so," said Don John; "only he can't be found. The bank directors did not discover the loss of the bonds till this afternoon. They were looking over the books all the forenoon, but were not able to find anything wrong. They counted the money and then began to examine

the securities. About a hundred men are looking for him now. I have been searching in the
mud and water, and I hope you will excuse me,
ladies, for coming before you in such a plight.
I was so busy that I forgot all about the meeting till just now, and then I could not spare the
time to go home and change my clothes."

"You are very excusable, Don John," replied
the president. "Have you seen Mollie Longimore?"

"I have not; but Prince Willingood told me
the family were almost beside themselves with
grief and terror."

"Poor Mollie! How I pity her!" added Minnie, wiping away the tears that dimmed her
bright eyes.

"It's a terrible hard case for the family," said
Don John, with emphasis.

"But it is not certain yet that Mr. Longimore will not return," suggested Minnie. "He
may have gone somewhere to obtain assistance."

"And taken forty thousand dollars in bonds
with him? That is quite impossible. The directors are certain that he has either run away
or committed suicide. I have not seen anybody

who believes anything else. Prince says Mrs.
Longimore and Mollie have no hope of anything
better, for the cashier had been worried for some
time. He is either dead or gone away ; and his
family are left without a dollar."

" How awful ! " exclaimed Eva. " Can't we
do something ? "

" Certainly we can," said Nellie Patterdale,
decidedly. " Every one of us loved poor Mollie
like a sister, and the family shall not suffer for
the want of anything."

This subject was discussed at considerable
length, and various plans were suggested for
assisting the family of the cashier in the most
delicate way possible, though the details were
not finally arranged. The abundant sympathy
of the girls for Mollie led them to believe that
they could furnish all the aid the stricken family
would need ; for they felt that if they could
raise over four hundred dollars for a boat, they
could obtain ten times that amount for so noble
and worthy a purpose as the care of the needy
ones. But they were young and enthusiastic,
with but little knowledge of the way of the
world. It was right to do such a deed, and it

seemed easy enough to them to accomplish it. This noble purpose begat a cheerfulness in the society, which, at last, brought their minds back to the boat.

"Don John, we were particularly desirous to see you this afternoon," said the president. "We wish to enquire about the boat which you have been building. Is it finished?"

"It is all done, and yesterday I had the name painted upon the stern, and on each side of the bow," replied the boat-builder.

"Indeed! What is the name?" inquired Minnie.

"DORCAS."

"That was an odd name for you to give to it."

"Not at all. I gave her the name of your society, and considering the use to which I intend to put her, it was the right thing to call her."

"Then you have a use for her?" asked Minnie, looking a little troubled.

"I have; and without any ceremony, allow me to present the boat to the Dorcas Society," said Don John.

"You cannot mean that," added the president, with a smile.

"I certainly do. I talked the matter over fully with the other member of our firm, — that's my mother, — and we agreed to present her to the society."

"But, Don John, we are able to buy the boat."

"Of course you are; and, thanks to the good people of this city, our firm is now abundantly able to present her to this society, which has done so much good to the poor," replied Don John, modestly.

"It is too much for you to give."

"Not at all; I built her wholly with my own hands, when I had nothing else to do. The stock did not cost much, and I hope you will not refuse to accept her, for any reason. As soon as I heard that the young ladies of this society wanted a boat, I decided to present her to you."

Certainly Don John desired to do this graceful thing for the sole sake of doing it, however the gift might serve him as a "business card." The boat was accepted by vote, and the thanks of the society presented to the donor.

"She will be ready for use by to-morrow, for the last coat of paint I put upon her is dry and hard," said the boat-builder.

"But who is to teach us how to row?" asked Eva.

"I move that Don John be invited to be our instructor in the art of rowing," said Ruth Hapgood; "I am sure he knows as much, or more, about it than anybody else."

This motion was carried with unanimity and enthusiasm by the society, and Don John accepted the delightful position thus assigned to him.

"Don John, what is the value of the Dorcas?" inquired Nellie.

"She has no value now; she is beyond price," laughed Don John.

"But what was the price you fixed for her?"

"When I had concluded to present her to the Dorcas society, she rose in value five hundred per cent. in my estimation. The pleasure of presenting her was worth at least a thousand dollars to me."

"But please answer my question. If you had wished to sell her, instead of giving her away,

THE PRESIDENT WAS NOT THE ONLY ONE WHO WEPT. Page 130.

what should you have asked for her?" persisted Nellie.

"I could not have sold her for any money, after I knew that this society intended to go into boating." replied Don John, who suspected that his fair friend wished, by some indirect means, to pay for the Dorcas.

"Didn't you say, a week ago, that you asked two hundred dollars for her?" demanded Nellie.

"That was before I knew you wanted a boat; and —"

"Was that the price of her?" interposed his questioner.

"It was; but —"

"No 'buts,' if you please, Don John. I wish to know for a special purpose, which in no way affects you."

"That was the price," replied the boat-builder, wondering what Nellie was driving at.

"Miss President."

"Miss Patterdale."

"I move that the society go into secret session," added Nellie.

"Is that a blow aimed at me?" asked Mr. Jelley.

"No sir; in consideration of the valuable
services you have rendered the society, as Mercury, *pro tem.*, you will be permitted to remain,
if you will pledge yourself not to reveal what
is said or done," said the president.

"I pledge my life, my fortune, and my sacred
honor, not to write, print, utter, say, reveal,
mention, hint, lisp, mark, dot, engrave, or indicate a word of what is said or done."

"It is well. Don John, as Mercury, you will
not disclose any of the private business of the
society," added Minnie.

"Certainly not."

The motion to go into secret session was
carried, and Nellie Patterdale had the floor.

"I move that two hundred dollars of the
money contributed for the boat be appropriated
to aid the family of Mr. Longimore," continued
she.

"Yes, yes, yes!" cried the girls, though
some of them had already thought that the sum
collected would enable them to purchase two
more boats, making three in all.

The appropriation was made without a dis-
senting vote. Minnie Darling was appointed a

committee of one to disburse the money as she thought best, but with instructions to do it privately, so as entirely to spare the feelings of Mollie and her mother. Nellie desired to use the rest of the boat money for the same purpose, but she thought it wise to defer any action in this direction till a future time, having some doubt whether or not it was proper to divert the funds from the purpose for which they were given.

"Now that we have one boat for our twenty-five members, we ought to arrange some plan by which we may all have an equal and fair use of her," said the president.

"How many will the boat hold, Mr. Instructor in the art of rowing?" asked Eva.

"Five, without any passengers," replied Don John. "I think you had better have only the regular crew while you are learning to row. Four at the oars, and one at the tiller lines, are the proper complement for the Dorcas."

"Then I think we had better divide ourselves into five clubs, each having its own name," suggested Nellie. "The first shall be the Dorcas Club, which shall also be the general name of the whole boating society."

The suggestion found favor with the girls,
and some time was spent in making the division.
The little rings of intimate friends formed the
bases of the several clubs, and the arrangement
was made without much difficulty. Mollie Longimore was the only member absent, and it so
happened that four of the five clubs were made
up at once, while one remained with only four
members. Naturally enough, the officers of the
society, who were its executive committee, and
were, therefore, together a great deal, united as
one club, and found themselves unable to obtain
another member.

"Mollie is absent," said Minnie. "Of course
she will not wish to row for some time, but we
will take her."

"O, yes," exclaimed Eva; "I am glad to
have her in our club."

"Now each club must have a leader," interposed Don John, when the division had been
made. "She will steer the boat, and be the
commander, the president of the club. Each
should elect its own leader."

The instructor in rowing thought this was
a better name for the chief than the one usually

applied to the office; and the girls separated in different parts of the room to ballot. In some of them several ballots were taken, before a choice was made; but in the officers' club, the four votes cast, without any electioneering or previous consultation, were for Mollie Longimore. The sympathy of the girls for their absent friend· was so deep and earnest, that they could not help manifesting it in all possible ways.

" Now, we have five clubs and only one boat," said the president; "and we must fix the time for each of us to use her."

" That will give one day in the week for each club," added Nellie: "and we have to attend the meeting of the society on Tuesdays, so that we cannot go on that day."

" That makes an easy thing of it," replied Ruth. " But suppose it should rain on any day?"

" The club for that day must loose its chance, I suppose," answered Nellie. " It will be as fair for one as for another, for it does not always rain on the same days of the week."

This arrangement was agreed to, and Don John suggested that the leaders of the clubs

draw lots for the days, which was also assented
to.   The instructor wrote the names of the days
of the week, except Sunday and Tuesday, on as
many slips of paper, which were to be drawn
from a book by the leaders.

"But we have no names yet," said Minnie.
"Which will be the Dorcas Club?"

"Yours," said several members; and the officers' club, of which Mollie was the leader, was
designated as the one . to retain the general
name of "Dorcas."

"What shall you call your club, Kate Bilder?" asked the president.

"The Lily," replied the leader.

"Very good.   Do you mean the tiger lily, the
lily of the valley, or the water lily?"

"We talked about those, but we liked 'Lily,'
simply, better than 'Water Lily.'"

"Suit yourself, Kate.   Now draw one of the
slips."

The leader of the Lily Club drew one of the
slips of paper from the book, upon which was
written the single word "Monday;" and the
secretary recorded the Lily's day.

"Jenny Waite, what is the name of your
club?"

" Fairy."

" Very well; draw."

" Saturday."

" Your name, Susy Thaxter? "

" Undine."

" Very appropriate; draw, if you please,"
continued the president.

" Wednesday."

" What shall we call your club, Carrie West?"

" Pysche."

" Draw."

" Friday."

" That's an unlucky day in the almanac of
the sailors, but I hope it will not prove so to the
Pysche Club," laughed Minnie, " As the leader
of the Dorcas Club, is not here, Eva will draw
the slip for her. It is Hobson's choice, and
Thursday is the only day not yet taken."

Of course Thursday was drawn for the Dorcas
Club. The business was hardly finished before
some one proposed to visit the boat-builder's
shop, to see the new boat, and in five minutes
more the party were on their way. Of course
the Dorcas was " perfectly splendid," and the
exclamation points were as thick as hail-stones
in a summer shower.

"O, I should like to see her on the water!" cried Eva Doane.

"It is a very easy matter to put her into the water," said Don John, prompt to take the hint. "But I want a little help, for she must be handled carefully. There comes Prince; he will assist me."

"You have bought the boat, I suppose," said Prince, after he had bowed to the young ladies.

"We have not bought her, but she has been presented to us," replied Minnie Darling. "Don John is as generous as a lord."

"Anything new about Mr. Longimore, Prince?" asked Don John willing to change the subject.

"His handkerchief was found on one of the wharves, and a small row-boat is missing from the same place," replied Prince gloomily. "They have dragged the water all about the wharf, but they can't find him."

"Whose boat was it?"

"I don't know; they have searched the whole water front of the city, without finding it," added Prince. "Some think he has gone off in the boat."

"He could not go a great way in a row-boat," said Don John.

"He may have gone out to drop himself into the deep water, and the boat drifted away. At any rate, if they can find the boat, it may afford some clew to him."

"Have you seen Mollie to-day, Prince?" inquired Nellie.

"Yes; after our house was burnt down last night, I staid at Mr. Longimore's; but I got up at seven o'clock, and left the house. I went to school as usual, and did not hear anything about Mr. Longimore till half past two. I went to his house then. Mollie had fainted away half a dozen times in the forenoon, but she was better when I saw her, though she was as pale as a ghost."

"Does she think her father is dead?" asked Minnie, the tears in her own eyes.

"She says she is almost sure of it; and if her father took the bonds at all, he must have been insane when he did so," continued Prince, sadly. "She says she is alone in the world now. I think some of you girls ought to go and see her."

"Let us go," Nellie proposed; but it was arranged that only she and Minnie should visit

10

her then; and they departed upon their mission of sympathy.

"I want to put this boat into the water, Prince," said Don John. "Lend us a hand."

Though Prince did not feel much interest just then in the boat or the Dorcas Club, he assisted to put the pretty barge in the water. She sat upon the tide like a fairy, as she was. The builder brought the oars, which were "spoons," made of pine, and very light.

"If the Lily Club will take their places, we will see how she works," added Don John.

"Goody! goody!" cried the members of that club.

"Steady!" shouted the instructor in rowing. "You will upset the boat, and tumble yourselves into the drink, if you board her in that style. When you get into a boat, you should do it as calmly as you would step on eggs. See where you are going to put your foot, and then put it there."

Don John helped the members of the Lily Club to their seats, and getting in himself, shoved the Dorcas far out from the shore.

"Before you do anything, young ladies, I

want to talk to you a moment," said he, smiling at the novelty of his position.

"What am I to do?" asked Kate Bilder, impatiently.

"You are to keep cool, and do nothing. When the girls can pull, you will steer," replied Don John. "Now you will each take an oar, if you please, and stand it up straight before you."

"Why, the oars are as light as a feather," said one of the crew.

"Well, I got them on purpose for you. They are made of soft pine, but they are strong enough, if you handle them carefully. Those who pull the starboard oars—"

"Starboard?" queried one of the fair rowists.

"The starboard is the right, and the port the left side of the boat, looking forward," explained the instructor, very patiently. "You are all sitting backward, so that the port oars are on your right, and the starboard on your left. I will give each of you a number. The after, or stroke, oar is No. 1. That's you, Maggie Bowen."

"Two," said Ella Haven.

"Three," added Julia Gray.

"Four," continued Louise Winn.

"Four is the bow oar," explained Don John. "The even numbers pull the starboard oars, and the odd the port oars. The starboard rowers will take the handle of the oar with the right hand, and the loom by the left."

"What is the loom?" asked Julia.

"An oar has three parts; the handle is the small part which you grasp in your hands; the blade is the flat part, and the loom is the portion next to the handle, which is inboard when you row. The port rowers will take the handle in the left hand, and the loom with the right. That's it. Now, Miss Bilder, you are the leader, and will give the orders. When she says, 'Boat your oars!' you will all drop your oars together into the boat, by the gunwale, or rail. Now!"

"Boat your oars!" said Kate.

Being the first time, of course it was done very clumsily.

"You should all drop them together," said Don John. "We will try that over again. When the leader says, 'Ready,' you will grasp the oars, as I told you. At the command, 'Up oars!' you will raise them all as one."

"Ready! Up oars!" repeated Kate Bilder; and the oars went up very well.

The two evolutions were repeated several times, till they were performed together.

"The next order will be, 'Let fall,'" continued the instructor, while the fair rowists held the oars up perpendicularly before them. "At the command, you will let the blade of the oar fall into the water, with the spoon, or curve at the end of it, turned up. As you do so, raise the handle, so that the oar shall not fall upon the gunwale. Slip it into the rowlock, and you are ready for business. Now try it."

"Let fall!" said the leader, who was a very apt scholar.

"Very well, indeed!" exclaimed Don John. "To get the oars back again to a perpendicular, the command is, 'Toss.' Try it again, if you please."

"Toss!" said Kate; and up went the oars.

"Capital!"

"Let fall!" added Kate; and she practiced the crew on all of the evolutions they had learned, till they did very well for beginners.

"Now we will pull a little; but I wish you

to take but one stroke in four movements. Place the oar so that the spoon is just out of the water. Push the handle away from you, at arms' length; this is one. Two, raise the handle just enough to sink the blade into the water, so as to cover the spoon. Three, pull. Four, drop the handle till the blade is out of the water."

Don John repeated his instructions several times, and then required each girl to do it alone, till she had the movement. After this they tried it all together, but the girls were so much excited when the Dorcas began to move through the water, that not much proficiency could be attained.

" Here endeth the first lesson," said the instructor, as soon as the rowers were able to pull a dozen strokes together.

The Lily Club returned to the shore delighted with this slight foretaste of the pleasures in store for them.

"It's real fun!" said Kate Bilder to her companions, who had been watching the experiment on the shore, as she joined them, and they walked towards home together.

CHAPTER VIII.

THE CASHIER'S FAMILY.

PRINCE WILLINGOOD had lost all the books he carried home in the fire, and if he had possessed any more clothes than those into which he had so hastily put himself when the alarm was given, he would have lost them. Having little or nothing to lose, he lost little or nothing by saving his uncle rather than his books, his two or three shirts, and a couple of pairs of coarse socks. It had never struck him so before, but doubtless he was fortunate in having so little to lose. Happy are they that have nothing to lose, for they shall lose nothing, and poverty has sometimes its compensating advantages, though, on the whole, it is not convenient and comfortable to be poor. Certainly no one would desire to be poor for the sake of escaping loss by fire. Of the brass kettle and the valubles in the cellar, Prince knew nothing, and therefore he had no regrets for them.

He waited till the fire had consumed the house in which the greater part of his cheerless life had been passed. There was nothing left of it but a few smouldering embers, which the firemen were drenching with water, and which were soon as black and cold as the night itself. Several of the neighbors had offered him the hospitality of their houses, and he had accepted that of the cashier, who showed him to the spare chamber of his unpretentious dwelling. He heard Mr. Longimore go out again, as he was getting into bed, and presently distinguished his voice and that of his uncle, as they spoke together in the street. He could not tell what they said, but he readily understood that the miser was bitterly bemoaning his loss, and probably the cashier was trying to comfort him. But Prince was tired, and he soon dropped asleep.

When he awoke in the morning, he heard the clock strike seven. He had intended to get up earlier, in order to ascertain, before he went to school, what his uncle desired to do in regard to his future residence, and to assist him, if he could. When he went down stairs, he was kindly greeted by Mrs. Longimore and Mollie, who had not before been aware of his presence in the house. Breakfast was all ready, and the family appeared to be waiting for the cashier. Prince said he would go and see what had become of his uncle.

"But don't go till after breakfast, Prince," interposed Mrs. Longimore. "It is all ready, and we are only waiting for father to come in."

"I thank you, Mrs. Longimore; but I think I will not remain," replied the young man. "My uncle may want me."

"He must be at the house of one of the neighbors, and he will stay there till after breakfast."

"No; I heard him say he should stay at the vacant house down the street."

"But that is not furnished; he could not stay there."

"I only know what he said."

"But there will be no breakfast there for you," persisted the good lady.

"Why can't you stay, Prince?" added Mollie. "We shall all be very glad to have you do so."

"And I will not keep you waiting," continued Mrs. Longimore, proceeding to place the breakfast upon the table. "We will sit down, and father will be here in a few moments. He sometimes goes over to the bank before breakfast; but he always comes home punctually at seven o'clock. I can't think what keeps him. Perhaps Mr. Bushwell wanted to see him about the fire."

Prince yielded to these pressing invitations, and partook of the meal with the family. When it was finished, Mr. Longimore had not appeared; but neither his wife nor his daughter felt any anxiety in regard to him.

"Our house is always open to you, Prince; and I hope you will stay with us till your uncle gets settled again," said Mrs. Longimore.

"Thank you; but I think the vacant house will be ready for us to sleep in by night," replied Prince, as he left the hospitable home of his friends.

He walked down the street to the dwelling where Fox Bushwell had taken refuge from the cold and the night. Mrs. Pining was already there; for as soon as she finished her breakfast, she hastened, with fear and trembling, to ascertain whether the money-lender was ruined or not, or whether or not the few hundred dollars which constituted all her worldly wealth was hopelessly lost. She was as miserable then as even Mrs. Pining could be, and her capacity for being miserable was immense. The pine bureau in the old house, which had contained her very limited wardrobe, had been burned. Even the note which Fox Bushwell had given her for the money he owed her was destroyed. She had had only time to save her own withered frame, when the alarm was given.

"Sufferin', dyin' world!" moaned she, as Fox Bushwell admitted her to the vacant house. "Everything's gone to ruin; and there ain't no hope o' nothing in this world."

"It isn't so bad as it might be, Mrs. Pining." replied Fox Bushwell. "I had a thousand dollars insurance on the house; and that's a thing I never had till about a month ago. But that isn't anything to what I've lost. It won't begin to cover the loss," he added as if troubled by a suspicion that he had admitted too much.

"There ain't no peace for the wicked in this world, goodness knows!" groaned Mrs. Pining, not much comforted by the words of the money-lender. "My two lace caps is both gone! I never wore 'em only when I went visitin'; and now I hain't got nothing to wear. My black gown I wore to Ezra's funeral is gone to dust and ashes, and I hain't got nothin' but the cal-liker I got on, when the smoke eena'most choked me. My stockin's, my flannel petticoat, and my wallet, with two dollars o' money in it, 's all gone, and I shan't git no good on 'em! Sufferin', dyin'! What are we comin' to?"

"I lost a good deal more than you have, Mrs. Pining. I don't know but I'm ruined — I can't tell yet. We must bear up in times of affliction, and try to be resigned."

"I can't be resigned; and tain't no use to try. Dyin' world! I hain't got nothin' left," groaned the widow, wiping the tears from her sunken eyes with the handkerchief found in the pocket of the "calliker." "You owe me four hundred dollars, Mr. Bushwell."

This last remark was hurled with energy at the head of the money-lender, while the old lady fixed a gaze of the most pitiful anxiety upon him. She did not say that the note had been burned; perhaps she knew her employer too well to make such a damaging admission.

"It isn't worth while to say anything about that just now," replied Fox Bushwell. "We are all in affliction. My house and all that I have are burned; but the Lord tempers the wind to the shorn lamb."

"You ain't the shorn lamb, Mr. Bushwell! I'm that creetur!" groaned Mrs. Pining. "I'm shorn of all my wool — my woollen stockin's, my flannel petticoat, my bombazine gown and — "

"We will not speak of those things now, Mrs. Pining. Trust in the Lord, and he will help you," replied the miser, evasively.

"I know that; but you told me that the Lord don't help nobody but those that helps themselves; and I want some o' that money you owe me, to buy some things with right off. Sufferin', dyin'! I hain't got nothing to wear!"

"I'm not ready to speak of such things yet. I'm in affliction; I'm suffering under a terrible loss."

"Don't you owe me four hundred dollars, Mr. Bushwell?" demanded Mrs. Pining.

"What if I do? I'm in no condition to pay it now."

At that moment Prince entered the room, and heard his uncle's reply.

"Did you hear that, Prince?" she asked, turning sharply upon the young man.

"Hear what?"

"What your uncle said."

"I did."

"You heard him say he owed me four hundred dollars — didn't you?"

"I heard him say what amounted to that," replied Prince, quietly.

"But I said I could not pay her now," protested Fox Bushwell.

"I don't want the whole on't now. I hain't had nothin' for two year; and I want the interest on't how."

"Very well; I will pay you the interest to-day or to-morrow, or as soon as I can get my insurance," whined Fox Bushwell.

"You hear, Prince," gasped Mrs. Pining. "Your uncle's note I had was burnt up in the fire; and I wanted to know how I stood."

"It was!" exclaimed the money-lender, with the feeling that he had been very weak in admitting the debt, though he had never given the housekeeper credit for the strategy she had exercised.

"Yes, it was; and two dollars o' money besides."

Fox Bushwell had admitted that he owed the money in the presence of a witness. It was too late to recede, and he did not attempt to do so.

"Uncle Bushwell, my books were burned, and some other things; and I should like my ten dollars for next month now," said Prince, when Mrs. Pining's case was settled.

"Ten dollars again!" gasped the guardian.

"For next month."

"This isn't the time to ask for money. I was burned out last night, and lost nearly everything I have in the world."

"Not quite so bad as that. You have money in the bank."

"I can't let you have it now."

"Then I must borrow it, which will compel me to say that I could not get the money of you," added Prince, who knew very well that his uncle's loss by the fire was trivial, compared with his possessions.

Fox Bushwell groaned and parleyed for some time, but at last he took the ten dollars from his pocket and gave it to his ward.

" What's going to be done, uncle Bushwell? " asked Prince, as he put the money away.

" I don't know yet. We must live in this house; and I shall lose the rent of it, or the chance to sell it, till I can build up the other. I heard yesterday that Captain Seeboard was going out west, and wanted to sell his furniture. I shall try to buy it, if he will sell it cheap enough," replied Fox Bushwell. " Everything's going to ruin with me. I don't know where I'm coming out."

" You haven't lost much, if the house was insured," added Prince.

" More than you have any idea of. I was poor before, and I'm poorer now."

" Were your papers burned, uncle? "

" Some of them were. I don't know yet what I have lost."

Fox Bushwell was not inclined to talk on this

subject, and Prince left him, to go to school. On the way, he bought new books and stationery, to replace what had been destroyed. His written exercises, prepared with so much care on that Monday evening, were all burned; but of course he was excused from the recitations, and, in the course of the day, he re-wrote them.

At recess the talk among the scholars was in regard to the fire, and Prince was obliged to answer the same questions a hundred times. Mollie Longimore was absent that day, and there were many inquries in regard to her, to which no one was able to reply. After school, Prince, concluding there would be no dinner in the new house for him, went to a restaurant for the meal. There, for the first time, he heard of the disappearance of Mr. Longimore. No one had seen him that day, and his keys of the bank and the vault could not be found. The porter had opened the rooms as usual, but no cashier had made his appearance. The president, who had duplicate keys of the vault, had been away, and did not return till noon, so that no business could be done before his return. Those in the saloon had not heard what transpired after the arrival of the president. ˋ (11)

Prince was thunderstruck at this intelligence, and hardly, by his eating, indorsed the dinner set before him. As soon as he had finished his meal, though he did not "finish" the food he had ordered, he hastened to the bank for further information. The directors had just completed their examination of the affairs of the institution. The books showed that the cashier's personal account was balanced; the cash was all right; but, on looking over the securities, it was found that the package of bonds was missing. This discovery seemed to explain the absence of the cashier.

The directors were wealthy men, and they were really more troubled by the fall of such a man as they had always believed the cashier to be than by the loss of the property. No one remembered to have seen the package for a month, and they could form no idea as to when it had been removed from the vault. No one knew of any speculations in which the cashier had been engaged, and no motive for his villany could be assigned.

Mr. Longimore was gone, and the bonds were gone. This was all that was known; but it was enough to satisfy the directors. In the mean time a diligent search was in progress for the missing cashier; but without any other result than has before been mentioned.

The first intimation of the stunning blow which fell upon the unhappy family of Mr. Longimore was given when the porter went to the house, at nine o'clock, to inquire where the cashier was. The poor wife and the terrified daughter — the only ones in that sad home who were old enough to understand and appreciate the possible calamity — were almost paralyzed when they learned that the father had not been at the bank since seven in the morning. Mrs. Longimore had not seen him since he went out to the fire at midnight. He had not come to his chamber after that event. She had seen the letter on the table, stamped, and directed to her husband's brother, which she had sent to the post-office immediately after breakfast. She had called in her neighbors for help, and her kind and sympathizing .friends had searched the city over for the absent one.

As soon as Prince had obtained all the information that was to be had at the bank, ho hastened to the home of the cashier, intent only upon assisting and comforting his family, with whom he had long been intimate. The fact that forty thousand dollars in bonds was missing had already been borne to Mrs. Longimore and her daughter; indeed, two of the directors had been there to search the house for them. The suspicion that the cashier had wrongfully appropriated the property was infinitely more terrible than the assurance of his death would have been to those loving ones. Mollie had fainted twice; but when Prince entered the house the effect of the shock had passed away, though the mother and daughter suffered hardly less, if their demonstrations were not so violent.

"I am glad to see you, Prince. Perhaps you can tell us something about him," said Mrs. Longimore.

"Indeed, I know nothing but what I have just heard at the bank," replied he gloomily. "I was never so shocked and astonished in my life."

"When did you see Mr. Longimore last?"

"I saw him at the fire; and he came up to the house with me. He showed me up to the room. That was the last I saw of him. He had some business with my uncle in the evening, and I signed my name as a witness to some papers which passed between them."

"What papers were they?" asked Mrs. Longimore, with interest.

"I don't know what they were; I didn't stop to read them.

"Then your uncle knows."

"Of course he does."

"I must see Mr. Bushwell at once,"

"Can I do anything to help you?" inquired Prince. "I am willing to do everything I can.'

"I wish you would go with me to your uncle," added the poor wife.

"I will, and he shall tell you all about the papers," replied Prince.

But before they left the house, Mr. Doane, the president of the bank, came in. Mrs. Longimore told him what Prince had said; and anything which promised to throw light upon the conduct of the cashier was full of interest. Mr. Doane decided to accompany them to the new home of the money-lender. They found Fox Bushwell and Mrs. Pining busily engaged in arranging a load of second-hand furniture, which had just been delivered at the house. The miser had bought out the contents of Captain Seeboard's house for a mere song, so anxious was the late owner of it to start for his new location in the west. The articles were very plain, and most of them much worn; in fact, they were not much better than those which had been destroyed in the fire of the night before.

"You seem to be very busy, Mr. Bushwell; but we must disturb you for a short time," said Mr. Doane.

"I can't stop for anything now," replied Fox Bushwell, furtively; and it must be acknowledged that the president of the bank was not a welcome visitor at the new home.

"We will not detain you long; and I think you and Mrs. Pining need a little rest."

"Sufferin', dyin'! Goodness knows I need it!" added the housekeeper.

"I heard that you had some business with Mr. Longimore last evening," continued Mr. Doane.

"I don't know that it concerns anybody but the cashier and me," whined Fox Bushwell.

"I don't know that it does; but you will find it for your interest, under present circumstances, to tell what it was," added the president, rather sharply, for he knew his man too well to stand upon any ceremony with him. "Some papers passed between you and him last evening."

"There wasn't anything wrong about that — was there?"

"I don't know yet. What were those papers?" demanded Mr. Doane.

"Well, you see, Mr. Longimore got into a little difficulty."

Fox Bushwell paused, as if doubtful whether it was prudent for him to proceed. Mrs. Longimore actually trembled with emotion, and wiped away the tears that blinded her eyes, for the money-lender's statement, so far, seemed to confirm her worst fears.

"What was the difficulty?" asked the president, sharply.

"He said he hadn't stole anything from the bank, or done anything wrong," mumbled Fox Bushwell.

"Did he say that?" exclaimed the poor wife.

"That's just what he said; and I don't believe he ever did anything out of the way."

"But what were the papers that passed between you?" repeated Mr. Doane, impatiently.

"I was just going to tell you. Mr. Longimore got into a little difficulty."

"You said that before."

"He has had a good deal of sickness in his family, and had to pay a good deal of money for doctor's bills."

"How well I know it!" sighed Mrs. Longimore.

"I don't believe in paying so much money to doctors. They can't do much good; and we are all in the Lord's hands."

"Will you tell me what the papers were, or shall I take the next step?" interposed the president. "You said Mr. Longimore got into a little difficulty. Now, go on."

"The long and the short of it is, he had overdrawn his wages. He owed the bank five hundred and twenty dollars. Mr. Longimore was honest; nobody can say he was not."

"I saw that his account had been balanced by the payment of five hundred and twenty dollars; and I found your check for that amount."

"I let him have the money, and he gave me

his note," added Fox Bushwell; he did not say for how much.

"What was the other paper?" demanded Mr. Doane, as if he had a right to know.

"That was the security he gave me," replied the money-lender, with a doubtful glance at the cashier's wife.

"What was the security?"

"I don't think that makes any difference."

Mr. Doane insisted upon knowing, and Fox Bushwell said that it was a bill of sale of the cashier's furniture and piano. Then the amount of the note was wrung from him; and the president was utterly disgusted.

"When did you see Mr. Longimore last?" asked he.

"I saw him at the fire."

"Was that the last time?"

"Well, no, it was not," whined the miser.

"When was the last time?"

"He came here about daylight this morning, to bring me a bundle of papers I left at the bank," replied Fox Bushwell, taking the package from his pocket.

Mr. Doane examined the papers very carefully, and assured himself that not a single bond was among them.

" What did he say to you ? "

" Nothing at all. He gave me the papers, and left right off."

" Did he say where he was going ? "

" Not a word; but I thought he looked and acted very wild," said the money-lender.

" Why did he bring you these papers at such a time ? "

" I don't know ; he said I might want them, I think. Then he went off."

Fox Bushwell stuck to his text, and the president left the house apparently satisfied. Mrs. Longimore could obtain no further information from him, and she went home, with the knowledge that the furniture and piano were to be taken from her in ten days. Prince went down to the boat-builder's, to assist him in searching for the body of the cashier.

CHAPTER IX.

WHAT THE DORCAS SOCIETY DID.

HOWEVER fascinated with boats the members of the Dorcas Society had become, they had no thought of abandoning the original object of the association, which was to do good to the needy. Their labors had not been confined to the perishing classes; to those who may be publicly assisted with food and clothing; but the society even had a precedent for its action in the case of the Longimores. A lady, who had supported her invalid mother by teaching in one of the public schools, was obliged to resign her situation on account of her own ill health. She was too proud to ask for help when her scanty means failed, but Nellie Patterdale, who had once been her pupil, called to see her, and discovered enough to satisfy her that her old teacher was actually suffering from want. She stated the case to the Dorcas Society, and a sum of money for the poor invalid was raised among the nabobs as privately as the boat money had been levied, and without the knowledge of the public, over a hundred dollars was placed in the hands of the invalid.

While the Lily Club were taking their first lesson in rowing, Nellie Patterdale and Minnie Darling called at the house of the cashier. Mrs. Longimore and Mollie were tolerably calm, though they had learned that even the furniture in the house was to be taken from them in a few days. Their eyes were red with weeping, but their tears had ceased to flow, and they seemed to be waiting for the calamity to spend itself upon them. Poor Mollie, without giving them expression, had begun to think great thoughts. While her mother was at Fox Bushwell's, she was considering the plan of obtaining young pupils on the piano, and she was sure that her friends would help her to obtain them. It was a relief to her to think that she could thus save her mother and the children from positive want. Her mother came back with the sad intelligence that every article of furniture in the house was owned by the money-lender, even to the piano, upon which she depended for the future. Though she might give the lessons at the homes of her pupils, she needed the instrument for her own practice. Under these circumstances, it was little that Nellie and Minnie could say to comfort Mollie and her mother.

"I cannot believe that my husband took those bonds," said Mrs Longimore. "It is less painful for me to believe that he is dead, than that he has done so great a wrong."

"I cannot believe it, mother!" exclaimed Mollie, trembling with emotion. "You do not believe it, Nellie?"

"I am not willing to believe it," replied Nellie. ?"

"My father was always so good and so kind! I am sure he would not do anything wrong. I know there is some terrible mistake. If the bonds are gone, some one else took them."

The visitors could not say anything. Without knowing much about the facts, they could not help feeling that appearances were altogether against the cashier.

"I can only hope for the best," added Mrs.

Longimore. "It appears that my husband had overdrawn his salary. He did not say anything to me, but he was terribly worried. Our expenses were very large during the winter, and he was in debt before. But rather than wrong the bank out of a single dollar, he borrowed enough of Mr. Bushwell to make himself square with the bank. I cannot think he would have done this, if he intended to leave, and take those bonds."

"It is very strange," said Nellie.

"No man was more devoted to his family than Mr. Longimore; but he gave a bill of sale of all the furniture in the house, rather than even seem to wrong the bank," pleaded the poor wife. "I cannot understand it."

"Did he sell your furniture?" asked Minnie Darling.

"I don't exactly comprehend the matter, but I believe that Mr. Bushwell can take everything we have in the house, if the note my husband gave is not paid in ten days."

"That is awful!" exclaimed Nellie, satisfied that even the Dorcas Society, with all its resources, could not meet so grave a case as this.

"I haven't a single dollar in the house, and our bills at the provision store and the grocery are unpaid," added Mrs. Longimore, with a shudder.

Nellie looked at Minnie, and the look was interpreted to mean, "Now is your time to act."

"We are very sorry," said Nellie, tenderly. "We have done nothing but think of Mollie since we heard what had happened."

"You are very kind, Minnie, to think of us. I don't know what will become of us. Mr. Bushwell is a hard man, and of course he will take all our things, if the money is not paid," added the cashier's wife. "Even if he don't, I have not the courage to send to the butcher and the grocer for what I know I have no means of paying for. I have no friends who are able to help me, but—"

The remark was cut short by the president of the Dorcas Society, who stepped up to Mrs. Longimore, and presented to her one of the white envelopes, which contained one hundred dollars. It was directed to the cashier's wife, and had been prepared to be delivered to her in the best way the circumstances would permit.

"What is this?" asked Mrs. Longimore, turning the envelope over very curiously, as though she feared it contained the news of an additional calamity.

"It will speak for itself; and I hope you will not be offended," added Nellie. "No one but our society knows anything about this business."

The afflicted lady opened the envelope, and took out the bills, and the note it contained, which she read. The tears flowed afresh from her eyes as she did so; and Mollie, when she saw the roll of bills, readily comprehended the meaning of the note. Perhaps she blushed; certainly she wept with her mother.

"I know not what to say," stammered Mrs. Longimore. "I was not prepared to ask for assistance, even of my husband's relatives, some of whom are in good circumstances."

"You have not asked for it; but it has come without asking," replied Minnie. "We are a thousand times happier to offer·you this aid than you can be to receive it."

"I do not feel willing to take this money," said Mrs. Longimore.

MRS. LONGIMORE RECEIVING THE PRESENT OF THE DORCAS SOCIETY.   Page 175.

"Do not, mother," added Mollie.

"You will grieve us very much if you do not," persisted Minnie.

Nellie related the whole story of the raising of the money for the boat, and of the vote appropriating a portion of it for the Longimores.

"You must take it," said Minnie, warmly. "We must do just what we are ordered by the society, and we have no power to take it back. We hope things will be brighter with you; and when you are able, you may return the money to the society."

"I will take it as a loan," answered Mrs. Longimore, when she thought again that, without it, her children must go to bed hungry.

"And you must not mention that you received it, for every one of our society is pledged to secrecy."

"You have removed one heavy load from my mind," replied the poor lady, wiping away her tears. 'If my husband is alive, he will surely return, and I shall consider this debt a sacred one."

"Don't do that; don't think of paying it,"

12

added Minnie. "We have more for you as soon as you need it."

"I am sure no one ever had such kind friends," sobbed Mollie.

"You must be as kind as they are, then, and permit them to do all they can for you. This is really the greatest kindness you can do them. All the girls love you, Mollie, and they pity you in your grief more than they can tell," said Nellie, taking the little hand of the troubled maiden.

"I did not think I should ever need your help," added poor Mollie.

"As you have done for others, now let others do for you," pleaded Nellie, as she and Minnie left the house.

In the street they met Prince, who was going home after the unavailing search for the body of the cashier. They asked him about the bill of sale; but he knew no more than the Longimores concerning the transaction. The cashier had agreed to pay one hundred dollars for the use of five hundred and twenty for ten days. The bill of sale was dated ten days ahead, and, without any further steps, the furniture would belong to the money-lender at the expiration of that time.

"But will your uncle take the furniture away from the poor family in ten days?" asked Minnie.

"I never knew him to let up on a debtor yet," replied Prince. "He is a Shylock, and would take the pound of flesh, if it were his due."

"It is awful to think of! Why, he will turn them out of house and home!"

"He is used to such things."

"But cannot something be done?" asked Nellie.

"I don't know; we will see. If I can prevent him from taking the things, you may be sure I should do so," said Prince, decidedly. "For my part, I don't see what is to become of the family. I hear that Mr. Longimore was in debt besides what he owed the bank; and I don't believe they have anything to live on."

Prince was really troubled about this matter. He wished he was twenty-one, and had his property in his own hands; he could solve the problem then without troubling any one. But he might as well try to squeeze milk out of a paving-stone as to get money enough for the occasion out of his guardian. Minnie looked at Nellie, and smiled.

"Shall I?" said she, mysteriously.

"Yes; he is our Mercury more than any other boy," replied Nellie.

Under the promise of secrecy, the president told him what the Dorcas Society had done. Prince was rejoiced; and, as he was a constant visitor at the house of the Longimores, he promised to look after them, and agreed to do whatever work they might require. He would have done all this without a suggestion from any one; but he was willing to give the Dorcas Society the entire credit of taking care of the sufferers.

It was quite dark when he reached the new home of his uncle. So hard had Fox Bushwell and the housekeeper worked during the afternoon, that the house was in condition to be occupied. The cooking-stove and the bedsteads had been put up, and the rest of the furniture placed. Supper was ready, and Prince partook of the meal with them. Though it consisted of tea, baker's bread and butter, it was better than usual, for Mrs. Pining had had no opportunity to spoil good "rye and Indian" by making them into loaves.

"What's the news, Prince?" asked Fox Bushwell as they seated themselves at the table.

"There is nothing more," replied the young man. "No trace of Mr. Longimore has been found."

"Somebody said his handkerchief had been found on a wharf, and that a boat was missing: is that so?"

"Yes; and the boat was kept at the wharf where the handkerchief was found," added Prince.

"I think there isn't much doubt that he has drowned himself."

"Why should he drown himself?"

"Because he had taken the bonds, and was afraid of exposure. I am inclined to think he was insane. He looked as wild as a hawk when he came to me in the morning," said the money-lender.

"If he drowned himself, do you suppose he had the bonds with him when he did so?" asked Prince.

"I don't know; I can't form any idea. It is the strangest thing I ever heard of in all my life."

"If he meant to run away, or commit suicide, why did he borrow that money of you to square his accounts with the bank?"

"That's what puzzles me," added Fox Bushwell. "I didn't want to lend him that money. I didn't feel safe to do it. I wouldn't have done it, if he hadn't helped me about my business."

"And he was to pay you a hundred dollars for the use of it for ten days?" queried Prince, who did not quite comprehend his uncle's way of doing a friend a favor.

"It was risky business, you see."

"When he gave you a bill of sale of his furniture?"

"That kind of security isn't worth much, Prince. Why, I gave only a hundred and fifty dollars for all I got of Captain Seeboard."

"Well, I should say that's all it's worth," added the young man, glancing around at the well-worn articles in the kitchen.

"I couldn't have bought it new for four

hundred. After I heard that Longimore had
gone off, I thought I would wait ten days, and
then his furniture will be mine, if the note
isn't paid; and it won't be now, of course.
But I can't afford to have such things in my
house as the cashier had, though I don't believe
they'll bring five hundred dollars at auction,
with the piano in the lot."

"How much would you lose then?" asked
Prince, quietly.

"The note is for six hundred and twenty."

"That is a hundred more than you lent him,"
added Prince quietly.

"It was his own offer. I didn't want to
lend him the money at any rate. It was too
risky," replied Fox Bushwell, in his whining
tones. "He said his brother would let him have
the money to pay me."

"Suppose he does not?"

"Then I suppose I must lose part of it."

"Shall you take the furniture?"

"Take it? Why not? I can't afford to lose
the debt."

"It would be to bad to take everything from
the house of the poor family."

"It would be too bad for me to lose the debt," retorted the money-lender. "I can't be sentimental when I've lost my house by fire."

If the young man had any doubts before in regard to the intentions of his uncle, he had them no longer. The wretch was ready to "clean out" the poor family as soon as the time came. The only hope for the Longimores was, that the cashier's friends in Portland would pay the debt. If they failed to do so, Prince was ready to do something to avert the catastrophe, though as yet he hardly knew how to proceed.

Mrs. Pining was very weary after her hard day's work, and she retired at a very early hour. Prince studied his lessons till nine o'clock, but he, too, was almost worn out by the loss of sleep the night before, and by the exertions of the day. Fox Bushwell did not seem to be at all exhausted, though he had slept less and worked more than any other member of that ill-assorted family. Two or three times he told his ward he had better go to bed; and he seemed to be very nervous and restless all the evening. At last, when he had finished his exercises, the young man lighted his lamp, and went up stairs.

The house, though more recently built, was the counterpart of the one which had been burned, and Prince's room was over the front stairs, while that of his uncle was the "parlor chamber." The young man retired; but the bed was even harder than the one which the fire mercifully consumed, and the situation was rather strange to him. He pondered the events of the day, and he felt very sad indeed when he thought of poor Mollie Longimore. Then he wished again that he were of age, and in possession of his own property. That furniture would not be taken then, and no such thing as want or privation should be known to the cashier's family. Mollie should smile again, and be happy as long as she lived, if money and his friendship could make her so.

No doubt he built up some very pretty air castles, as he lay wondering why he did not go to sleep, when he had been so sleepy; but whatever gilded fabric his fancy conjured up, the fair Mollie was there to people it, and to be the central figure of every picture.

Prince could not sleep, perhaps because he had retired an hour earlier than usual. At last the clock struck ten, when he thought it must be midnight. He turned over, and addressed himself again with renewed vigor to the task of going to sleep. But there were no poppies in his pillow.

While he was thus wrestling with Somnus and and Morpheus, he heard, or thought he heard, a sound like that of a hammer striking against brick-work. He rose in the bed, and listened The sound was repeated again and again, and it was certainly in the house. He got out of bed, and partially dressed himself. He feared that some villains were trying to break into the house. Perhaps some wretches, suspecting that Fox Bushwell had a large sum of money by him, intended to rob him. He had not heard his uncle go to bed; and, lighting his lamp, he entered the front chamber. The old man was not there; and still the noise of the hammer, or whatever it was, came up from the lower part of the house. Leaving the lamp in his room, and closing the door, he carefully descended the stairs in his stocking feet. He soon satisfied himself that the noise came from the cellar. He crept softly into the kitchen, after he had assured himself that his uncle was not there. Then he heard the sounds more plainly than before. Some one was at work on the rear chimney in the cellar — the one that passed up through the kitchen.

As his uncle was not in the sitting-room, nor in the kitchen, nor in his chamber, Prince concluded that it must be he who was at work at this unseemly hour; doubly unseemly to one who had been hard at work all day, and could hardly have slept any the night before.

Probably Prince was not very different from other boys of his age, and not very different from mother Eve herself, for his curiosity was excited. He wanted to know what his uncle was doing at that time of night. He had heard it said that Fox Bushwell had partly learned the mason's trade, when he was young, and he had himself even seen him lay bricks. While he was creeping towards the cellar door, in order to obtain a better view of the operations of his uncle, he stumbled over a stick of wood, which lay on the floor near the stove. The spell was broken and he retreated to the sink, on the other side of the room, just as the untimely workman rushed up stairs, and discovered him in the act of drinking from the tin dipper he had taken from the water-pail; not that he was any more thirsty than a boy always is, for the act was only a piece of strategy.

" What are you doing here, Prince ? " demanded Fox Bushwell, evidently terrified by the sight of his ward.

" Getting a drink of water," replied Prince. " What are you doing in the cellar ? "

" This back chimney is out of order, and I was fixing it. There's a hole in the flue down cellar, which spoils the draft," answered the money-lender.

" It's rather late to do such a job," suggested Prince.

" I was too tired to do it before ; and I had to do it to-night, or the house will be full of smoke when the fire is made in the morning," the old man explained.

Prince appeared to be satisfied, though he could not help thinking that his uncle had not seemed to be very tired, only nervous and rest-

less during the evening. He went to bed, and
was soon asleep. When he came down the next
morning, his guardian had gone out to get something for breakfast, and Prince visited the cellar
in order to see what had been done to the chimney. The rear one — larger than the other —
was built on an arch, which was now filled with
old lumber. He could find no place where a hole
had been stopped, though there were a pail of
mortar and some pieces of bricks on the floor.
He removed some of the lumber from the arch,
and, within a foot of the floor, he found that
two bricks had been recently laid, for the mortar was soft and green.

He did not believe that a hole in that place
could have affected the draught of the flue; he
was more inclined to believe that his uncle had
opened out a hiding place for some of his valu-
ables. But, whatever he had done, the matter
did not concern him; and after breakfast he
went to school as usual.

CHAPTER X.

THE UNDINE CLUB.

FOX BUSHWELL appeared to be the last person who had seen Mr. Longimore, though a storekeeper thought he had observed a man who looked like him going down the main street about sunrise. A small steamer had been sent to explore all the shores of the bay in the vicinity of the city, to discover, if possible, the missing boat, in which the cashier was supposed to have left the wharf; but it returned in the evening without having obtained any clue whatever to it. On Wednesday the directors of the bank sent for Fox Bushwell, and examined and cross-questioned him to their satisfaction; but he still told his story just as he had related it to the president. The cashier had come to the house at daylight in the morning, and given him the bundle of papers he had left at the bank.

"What did he say when he brought them to you?" asked Mr. Doane; and he had put the same question to him half a dozen times before.

"He said I might want the papers," replied Fox Bushwell. "He looked and acted wild. That's all I know about it, as I have said before."

"But didn't you ask him any questions?"

"No, sir, I did not. I hadn't any time to say anything before he was gone."

"Didn't you think it was very strange that he should come to you so early in the morning?" inquired one of the directors.

"Yes, I did; I thought it was very strange. And he looked and acted so wild that I was going to ask him what the matter was; but he went off before I could do so."

"What did you think was the matter with him, Mr. Bushwell?"

"I hadn't time to think much about it, he was off so quick. I knew he was in trouble, for I lent him the money the night before to make his account good with the bank. He was worried, and I didn't think so much about his conduct in the morning as I should if I hadn't seen him the night before."

"Could you think of any reason why he brought you those papers at that early hour?" asked Mr. Doane.

"I couldn't then, but I can now," replied the money-lender, warily.

"Well, what reason do you assign for it?"

"He knew he was going off, if I did not, either to clear out or to make way with himself; and I suppose, after the fire, he thought I might want the papers, for my insurance policy was among them," replied Fox Bushwell; and, though he had begun with a more manly tone than he generally used, he had now come down to the peculiar whine which seemed to be a part of his miserly nature.

"Didn't he know you could get the papers yourself when you wanted them?" inquired a director.

"He helped me about some of my business, and I left the bundle of papers in his charge. He made up the package just as he did the papers belonging to the bank. Perhaps he thought the directors would not let me have the papers; or, as they were left in his care, that he ought to return them to me, before he went off. I don't know what he thought; I can only guess at it; and you can guess for yourselves as well as I can."

"Which way did Mr. Longimore go, when he left your house?"

"He went up the street towards the bank."

"Were you awake when he came?"

"No; I was asleep in the front room — but not very sound asleep. His step woke me; and when I heard him knock, I went to the door. I thought it likely it might be my boy Prince. As soon as I opened the door, he handed me the papers, and said I might want them. Then he turned round, and hurried down the stairs. I was going to ask him what the matter was; but he didn't give me time. I have told you all this about a dozen times; but I'll keep on telling it all day, if you say so."

Perhaps there was something in the manner of the money-lender which excited the suspicions of the president of the bank; if there was, he found nothing to verify them. Fox Bushwell's story was very simple, and he did not vary it in the slightest particular. He was one of those prudent witnessess who believe it is better to

13

know too little rather than too much. Mr.
Doane and his associates inquired into the business transaction of the preceding evening, and the
money-lender told the whole truth without
reserve. He exhibited the note and the bill of
sale, and everything appeared to be regular.
The bank officials were unable to obtain a single
fact which threw any additional light upon the
singular conduct of the cashier. He was gone,
and the bonds were gone. He was "rather wild"
when last seen, which tended to strengthen the
belief that he had drowned himself in the bay.

"I am pretty well satisfied that he has made
way with himself," said Captain Hapgood.

"Where are the bonds, then?"

"I can't tell. He may have used them up in
some stock speculation."

"But there would be something among his
papers to indicate it, if he had — some letter or
memorandum."

"If he was shrewd enough to square his
accounts with the bank, he was smart enough
to burn his letters and other papers. It is very
strange, I know; but I can think of no other
explanation of his conduct." added the captain.

"If he had drowned himself, the boat would have been found before this time," suggested a director.

"I have a theory in regard to that, which came to my mind last night while I was thinking of the affair," continued Captain Hapgood. "Mr. Longimore, according to all accounts, was full of trouble, and rather wild. Crazy people are always cunning. My theory is, that he pulled over to one of the rocky shores, filled his boat with stones enough to sink her when the water was let in, and then went out into deep water again. I fancy that he tied himself down to the boat, or crawled under the thwarts, and then pulled the plug out of the bottom of the boat. If he did this, of course neither the boat nor his body will come up to tell what has become of him."

"All that is only a supposition," said Mr. Doane, with a smile at the ingenuity of the explanation.

"It is only what might have been, I know. If he has run away, the boat would certainly have been found," persisted Captain Hapgood.

Though this theory did not satisfy any person,

no more plausible one could be suggested. Fox Bushwell left the bank with a feeling that he had conducted himself prudently, and that he had succeeded in all he had undertaken. Day after day passed away, and no intelligence of the absent cashier came. The police in all the large cities were on the lookout for him, and officers employed by the bank were searching the surrounding country. Mrs. Longimore gladly accepted the theory that her husband's troubles had made him insane, and that he had drowned himself in the bay ; for it was better to believe this than to think that, in his right mind, he had stolen the property of the bank. She and her daughter mourned him as dead, and theirs was a sad, sad home. Two or three times a day Prince Willingood called upon them, and they allowed him, at his own urgent request, to do the work about the house which the absent father had done. They spoke to him freely of the darkened future, which had hardly a ray of hope for them.

On the third day after the disappearance of the cashier, came a letter from his brother to Mrs. Longimore. He had heard, of course, of the " irregularity " of her husband, and he had

received the letter addressed to him, imploring
aid to save the cashier from disgrace and ruin.
He could do nothing ; he had just failed in business, and enclosed in his letter a slip cut from
a daily paper, containing the legal proceedings
in his case. This hope was cut off. The mother and
her daughter wept afresh at this bad news. The
brother expressed his sympathy, and this was all
he could do. Prince read the letter, and listened
to the sobs of Mrs. Longimore and Mollie as he
did so. He tried to comfort them, but he was
powerless to do so.

"You shall not want for anything, Mrs. Longimore," said Prince, confidently. "I know
what the girls have done; and before the money
they loaned you is gone, some way will be provided for you to live. Mollie shall give lessons
on the piano, and — "

"But the piano is no longer ours."

"My uncle shall not take it," protested Prince,
warmly. "I can obtain the pupils, I know.
Do not weep; all shall be well in time. You
can take boarders, open a store, or keep a
school," suggested the young man.

"We might take boarders," replied Mrs. Longimore, thoughtfully, and with a gleam of hope,

"But you need not do anything yet a while. Do not be worried. I wish I was twenty-one!" added Prince, with an enthusiasm which had its effect on the mother and daughter.

He went home; but his presence and his words had kindled a hope. He left the skies less black behind him, though he was puzzled to know what he could do, with all his worldly goods locked up in the hands of his miserly uncle.

After school on Wednesday, a special meeting of the Dorcas Society had been called, and Don John, the boat builder, had been invited to be present. The enthusiasm for boating was at the highest pitch. The experience of the Lily Club had been so delightful that the other clubs could hardly wait till their days came. The meeting was called to order at three o'clock, for the Undine Club were to have the boat at four.

"The princely generosity of Don John has left us sufficient funds to procure another boat," said Nellie Patterdale, when the society was called to order.

"We need another," added Eva Doane.

"Wouldn't it be nice if we could have five

boats, so that we could all go every day!" exclaimed Kate Bilder.

"Perhaps we may have them by and by," replied Nellie; "but I think a couple will do very well for the present—at least till we have all learned to row."

"I move that we buy another boat at once," said Jennie Waite.

"Second the motion," added Kate Bilder.

"I offer an amendment, that Don John be employed to build one like the Dorcas," interposed Nellie.

"I accept the amendment," added Jennie. "But how long will it take to build one?"

"Don John can answer that question," said Minnie, turning to the boat-builder.

"I might do it in three weeks, if I employ help enough; perhaps in two," answered Donald.

"We can't wait so long," protested Kate.

"There is a four-oar boat for sale in the city, the one I used as a model for the Dorcas," added Don John. "She was built last year, and the price is two hundred dollars."

"Let's buy her!" cried Jennie.

" I think we can wait two or three weeks," said Nellie.

" I'm sure we can't."

" Yes, Jennie Waite," laughed Minnie.

" It would be such fun to have two boats!" exclaimed Kate. " We could get up a race. Let us buy her at once."

" I hope we shall not do so," continued Nellie. " After such a magnificent present, I think we can wait two or three weeks for Don John to build the boat."

" O, yes, certainly we can. I didn't think," added Jennie, blushing.

All of them saw that it would be very swinish to purchase a boat, instead of giving an order to Don John to build one, after his generous gift of the Dorcas ; and not another word was said about buying the one that was for sale.

" Question!" shouted the members.

" The motion is to employ Don John to build another boat," said the president.

" I beg permission to say a word," interposed Donald. " If the members prefer to purchase the boat, I hope they will do so, and not wait two or three weeks in order to give me the job. It will not make any difference to me whether I build her or not. I expect to lay the keel of a large schooner-yacht in the course of two or three weeks; and I shall have enough to do."

"Question!" repeated the girls.

The motion was carried unanimously.

"Don John, you will build the new boat at once," said the president.

"Of course I will do so, Miss President, if such is your order, for I would swallow my own head rather than disobey you," replied the representative of the firm of Ramsey & Son.

"Such is our order."

"Then I obey; but I shall be compelled to resign my pleasant position as instructor in rowing to the Dorcas Club.

"Resign?"

"I must employ one or two men to help me build the boat; and I must work upon it myself, instead of sunning in the smiles of these water nymphs."

"Very pretty!"

"This is a business matter; and if I do not

attend to it, the boat may not be ready as soon as I wish, and certainly not as soon as you wish," added Don John. "Please to accept my resignation, and I will try to have the boat in the water in ten days, if I have to work nights upon her."

"But whom shall we get to teach us?" asked Nellie.

"There are plenty of rowists who understand the business better than I do."

"Who?"

"Prince Willingood, for one."

"Prince!" "Prince!" shouted several of the girls.

"I move that the resignation of Don John be accepted," said Eva; and the motion prevailed.

Prince was then elected to this highly important position, and Don John was requested to inform him of the will of the club. The business of the meeting was completed, and the Undine Club, who were entitled to the use of the boat on that day, hastened to the shop of the builder, where she was kept. Don John, who was to instruct them on this occasion, pro-

ceeded as he had done the day before, until the
girls were able to pull a stroke together. The
Dorcas darted off, for it required very little
power to move her. Though the members of
the club flattered themselves that they could row
as soon as the boat began to move, their stroke
was very awkward and uneven, and the fair
rowists were likely to exhaust their strength in
pulling a single mile. Already they puffed like
so many seals.

"Ready to lie on your oars!" said Susie
Thaxter, the leader, as instructed by Don John.
"Oars!"

At the last command, the girls leveled their
oars at the proper distance above the water.

"What is the matter?" asked one of the
rowers.

"Nothing," replied the instructor.

"What have we stopped for?"

"It is about time for you to begin to learn
how to row," laughed Don John.

"I thought we were rowing."

"I didn't think so. You were sort of paddling and beating the water with the oars; but
the water can stand it a good deal better than

you can. You are all puffing like porpoises."

"But we went real fast."

"Too fast for beginners; you will wear yourselves out in half an hour, and at this rate the exercise will do you more harm than good," said the boat-builder, gravely. "I want you to understand that I am duly and properly impressed with the responsibility of my position as professor of the art of rowing."

"Professor Ramsay!" laughed Susie.

"Thank you; I accept the title as proper and fitting, and regret that I am so soon to vacate the chair," added Don John. "While I retain it, I desire faithfully to discharge its duties. Ladies should do everything gracefully; therefore you should row gracefully. But allow me to add that you row like so many sand-crabs, sidling about in search of their breakfast."

"By all means, let us row gracefully," said Kitty Jones.

"Moreover, it becomes my duty to insist that you shall row easily," continued Professor Ramsay. "You make harder work of it than a hod-carrier, who has to shin up a ladder with fifty bricks on his shoulder, and possibly one in his hat. So much hard work will tire you out, and impair your health. Pardon me for this long speech; but consider the heavy responsibility resting upon me."

"We are all willing to learn, Don John, if you will only tell us what to do," added Susie.

"In the first place, then, you must sit up straight, and throw your shoulders back, just as you do in the calisthenic exercises. In the second place, you must inflate the lungs when you gather up for the stroke. In position, if you please."

The girls straightened up, and threw their shoulders back. They made the movements, with the breathing exercise, a few times till they got the idea, without dipping the oars.

"That will do very well. All of you dip the blades too deep in the water, which very much increases the labor. Now, oblige me, at the word, by pulling a few strokes, only half covering the blade."

"Ready —give way together!" said the leader, at the instructor's request.

"Dip lightly. Too deep. Only half cover the blade of the oar — just bury the spoon, and no more. Very well indeed. But you lift the oars too high above the water when you gather up; that is, at movement No. 1. Just clear the water, and no more. Slowly; don't hurry. No, no! that's too fast. — Stop them, Susie."

"Ready to lie on your oars! Oars!" called the leader; and they all ceased as one, and came into the proper position.

"You must do it very slowly. I will call the movements by number — one, two, three, four; one, two, three, four. No faster than that. Now, try again. — Give the word, Susie."

After considerable practice, Don John taught them to row very slowly and steadily. Taking out a long led pencil, he beat the time, like the conductor of an orchestra. The rowists were so interested in the exercise, that they made remarkable proficiency.

"Now I wish to make it still easier." Professor Ramsay proceeded, when the club ceased rowing again.

"I don't see how it can be any easier," said Kitty.

"O I wish you to be able to pull a couple of miles without being at all fatigued: and you

can, when you get used to it. Now I will give
the time in six beats, instead of four. Three will
come on the stroke, as before; but on the fifth
and sixth beats you will lie on your oars. This
is the man-of-war stroke. Are you all ready?"

"Ready."

"One — two — *three* — four — five — six. No;
you are all in a snarl!" laughed Don John.
"Rest on five and six. Now try again. One—
two — *three* — four — five — six. That's better."

The exercise was repeated until the rowists
were accustomed to the movement, and they
made the rest after the stroke without breaking
the time. Of course the length of the stroke,
and the dip, were often corrected; but even the
professor was astonished at their progress.

"I hope you are satisfied," said Kitty.

"Not quite. You must now learn to feather
the oar, and never pull a stroke without doing
so," replied Don John. "On four, as you lift
the blade of the oar out of the water, turn it,
so that it shall rest flatwise, near the surface of
the brine."

The instructor took an oar, and showed how
it was done. Then each girl practiced till she

could do it. In half an hour the Undine Club returned to the shore, and astonished the other clubs by the ease and grace with which they pulled. As instructed, the bow oarswoman shipped her oar, and stood by the boat-hook, as the Dorcas approached the landing-place. Everybody was satisfied, and Don John not the least so.

CHAPTER XI.

THE NEW PROFESSOR OF ROWING.

TO the members of the Dorcas Society, the most favored place of resort, after dinner, was the boat-shop of Ramsay & Son, where Don John and Kennedy, his workman, were getting out the frame of the Lily, as the new boat was to be called. When they arrived, a new surprise awaited them; for, by the side of the Dorcas lay the very counterpart of her, with the name "Undine" painted upon the stern, and each side of the stem.

"Whose boat is that, Don John?" asked Susie Thaxter, the leader of the Undine Club. "Somebody has stolen our name, and I don't think it's fair."

"It is wicked to steal," replied Don John, his eyes twinkling with mischief.

"Somebody took that name just because we

14

did," pouted Susie. "If it was any of the boys,
I never will speak to them again!"

"It was very naughty," added Don John.
"The boat was sent here early this morning,
and I was directed to have the name 'Undine'
painted upon her in three places, as on the Dorcas. You know that I can only obey orders,
even if I break owners. If I had been ordered
to paint 'Susie Thaxter' — "

"Paint Susie Thaxter! Paint me!" laughed
the merry girl.

"I was going to say something more. I know
you don't paint; your cheeks are as red as a
ripe peach. If I had been ordered to paint
'Susie Thaxter' on that boat, I should have had
it done."

"Of course you would. That would have
been more sensible than stealing the name of
our club; for I hope we shall have a boat some
time."

"I hope you will; and as I can build two
boats at the same time about as quick as I can
one, I shall get out a pair of them. I shall
have two men at work for me to-morrow."

"But who owns that boat?" asked Kitty
Jones.

"I am sure I don't know who owns her now. It is the one I spoke to you about, yesterday, as being for sale. She was sent here this morning, with a note from General Jones — "

"My father!" exclaimed Kitty.

"From your father. I was ordered to paint the name 'Undine' upon her, and send the bill to him," replied Don John. "This afternoon a letter was left in my care for the president of the Dorcas Club, which I was requested to deliver when the girls came down to row. Here it is."

"Minnie Darling hasn't come yet, but she will be here soon. The Undine is a very pretty boat," added Kitty.

"I built the Dorcas after her model, as I told you; and the two are as nearly alike as two peas. The Lily will be precisely like them," said Don John.

"What are you going to do with the other one you are building?" asked Susie.

"That's an open question. I have not decided yet; but from the interest taken in boating, I am sure there will be a market for her, and perhaps for half a dozen more."

"Here are Minnie and Nellie," said Kitty, anxious to know the contents of the letter.

The boat-builder delivered the missive to the president, who opened and read it. As she did so, a smile lighted up her face, and her companions were sure that it contained pleasant intelligence.

"What is it, Minnie?" demanded Susie, impatiently.

"Listen, and I will read it," replied Minnie: "'Mr. Edward C. Jones presents his compliments to the Dorcas Boat Club, and requests the association to accept, as his gift, the four-oar boat to which he has given the name of UNDINE, with his best wishes for the health and happiness of the members, and with the hope that the boat will contribute something to the enjoyment of the coming season.'"

"Goody! goody!" shouted several of the girls, in their enthusiasm.

"You tell your father he is just the nicest man on record, Kitty," said Susie. "How did he happen to do this magnificent thing?"

"I'm sure I don't know. After tea last evening, I was telling mother and the rest of the folks; what an elegant time we had had, and what splendid rowists we had become, and how nicely Don John instructed us, so that it was easier to row than it was to sit still, and how hungry I was when I got home, and how we were to row gracefully as well as easily, and what fun we should have all summer, and that Don John was going to build another boat, and how I wished we had boats enough for all the girls — "

"And by that time I suppose your father was half crazy, because you talked so fast," laughed Nellie Patterdale.

"No, he wasn't. He was reading his newspaper, and he didn't seem to mind what I was saying. I told the folks that some of the girls wanted to buy the boat that was for sale, and if I had money enough, I'd buy her myself. Father didn't take a bit of notice of what I said."

"It seems that he did."

"Well he didn't ask me even a single question," added Kitty.

"Evidently there was no need of any questions," said Minnie; "for you told all you knew and all you felt without being asked."

"I don't care! I never enjoyed myself half so much before, as I did in the boat yesterday afternoon. Mother was afraid I should hurt myself rowing, and said it was too hard work for girls. Then I told her everything Don John had said about making easy work of it, and that I wasn't a bit tired after we learned to row. Then to think that father heard all I said, and went off this morning and bought this boat, and gave it to the Dorcas Club! Now each of the clubs can go twice a week, instead of once, and next week will be vacation."

"You can use her this afternoon, if you like, only you must be careful not to rub the letters that are painted on her," suggested Don John.

"That will be nice!" exclaimed Kitty. "The Psyche Club can have her."

"But we have not learned to row," said Carrie West, the leader of the club mentioned. "We must be instructed before we can go out, and the professor is to go with the Dorcas Club, who have the boat to-day."

"Where is Prince?" asked Minnie.

"He will be here very soon," replied Don John. "It isn't four o'clock yet."

"Can't you go with the Psyche Club, Professor Ramsay?" asked Kitty.

"I cannot; if I do, Kennedy must stop work as well as I, and we can't get these boats done at the time stated. Please don't call me professor any more; I abdicate in favor of Prince Willingood, who has been chosen as my successor. Transfer the title to him; he is worthy to bear the laurel and bear the honor," laughed Don John. "Besides there will be so many professors around, that we shall not know one from another. The barber is a professor, and so are the horse-doctor, the bumpologist, and the lightning-rod man."

"Here is the Simon Pure professor," said Susie Thaxter, as Prince made his appearance.

"The what?" demanded the new instructor in rowing.

"The professor, Prince; you are the professor of the art of rowing."

"Am I, indeed?" chuckled Prince. "I'm a greater man than I thought I was; and I beg to express my warmest thanks for the distinguished honor conferred upon me. I will endeavor to discharge my arduous duties with fidelity and discretion, and thus to win the favor of those who have placed me in this honorable and useful position. Allow me to add that Don John has fully instructed me in regard to his system of rowing, and I shall follow his method."

Both of the boats were put into the water, and hauled up alongside the little pier which Don John and his man had built in front of the shop.

"But which club is going in the Undine?" said Minnie, as she seated herself at the stroke oar.

"The Psyche, of course," replied Kitty. "It is their next turn."

"But we can't row," added Carrie West.

"And for that reason, I hope the Psyche Club will not go out in the Undine, for they will only contract bad habits," said Prince.

"Miss President, I move, as the sense of the club, that the Undine Club, knowing how to row, ought to use the second boat," continued Nellie, at the bow oar of the Dorcas.

"Just my opinion, exactly," cried Prince. "Then the Dorcas Club can see just how to

row, and their example will make our work all
the easier."

Minnie put the question to vote, and the
motion was carried.

"I think it is real mean, there!" said Kittie,
impulsively. "Neither the Psyche nor the Fairy
Club have been in the boat yet. I would rather
have them go than go myself."

"But we can't row," persisted Carrie West.
"I'm afraid we should tip over, or spoil the
boat."

"I don't want to go till Prince can go with
us," added Jennie Waite, the leader of the Fairy
Club.

So said all the members of the two clubs
which had not yet been in the boat.

"We had much rather see your club row,
Kitty," continued Carrie West. "I enjoyed
looking at you, yesterday afternoon, quite as
much as I should rowing myself. Your movements were the very poetry of motion."

"That's so!" cried Prince. "I must have
the Undine Club as a model for the Dorcas."

Kitty, over-persuaded, gave up the point. As
her father had presented the boat to the club,

she wanted the members to feel that she belonged
to all, and not to her particular club. The members of the Undine Club took their places, Susie
Thaxter being in the stern-sheets with the tiller-
ropes in her hands.

"Ready! Up oars!" said she. "Shove off!"

The last order was properly addressed to the
bow and stroke oarswomen, whose duty it was
to shove the boat out from the pier; and, having done so, to elevate their oars, in readiness
to "let fall" with the others; but Don John
did this part of the work for them, and pushed
the Undine far out from the shore.

"Let fall!" said the leader; and all the oars
dropped into the water as one, with the blades
athwartships. "Give way together!"

The Undines began to pull with a very slow
and measured stroke, making the long pause
when the oars were raised out of the water.
But slow as the stroke was, the boat went ahead
quite rapidly, for she was very sharp and very
light. A stout boy, without much expenditure
of force, could have rowed her even faster than
she was going, and this slight amount of muscle,
divided among four girls, made it very easy

indeed for them. Don John had positively for-
bidden them to row any faster than the time
he had given them, and Prince had repeated
the order as they started.

The fact was, that Dr. Darling, Minnie's
father, who was a wealthy retired physician, had
been to see Don John as soon as he learned
the latter had been chosen as instructor. He
had given the young professor some excellent
advice in regard to physical exercise for girls,
and had especially cautioned him not to allow
them to make hard work of it. The points of
this lesson had been duly handed over to
Prince.

The girls on the shore clapped their hands
when the Undine went off, so pretty and graceful were the movements of the rowers; and the
Dorcas Club watched them for some time. It
soon appeared that there were other spectators,
for quite a number of the friends of the girls
were coming down to the shore. Among them
was Dr. Darling, who commended Don John's
system of rowing in the highest terms. But the
Dorcas Club were not anxious to make their first
attempts in the presence of an audience, and

Prince paddled the boat away from the shore, and behind a wharf, before he commenced his lesson. As his predecessor had done, he explained very fully what he wished to accomplish, and then taught the club the movements. The girls were apt scholars, and in an hour they pulled a very pretty stroke, precisely like that which Don John had given to the Undines.

"You are doing bravely," said Prince. "You can row almost as well as Kitty's club now."

"Then I think we may go in and show ourselves," laughed Minnie. "My father is on the wharf, and I suppose he wants to know whether we are killing ourselves or not."

"Very well; we will go as closely to the shore as we can by Don John's wharf," replied Prince. "Don't dip too deep, if you please."

"But we don't more than half cover the blades," said Nellie, who knew something about rowing herself.

"I don't wish you to dip any deeper at present. I know the rule is to cover the blade, and we shall do so by and by. We must begin very gradually, for none of you are used to hard work. As you are strengthened by exercise, we will dip deeper."

"Here comes the Undine," added Minnie. "How prettily they row!"

"You are doing about as well as the Undines; only keep cool, and don't hurry. One — two — *three* — four — five — six. Not faster than that," continued Prince.

The two boats came alongside of each other, both pulling the slow and measured stroke, which made their speed exactly the same. The instructor acted as leader, in the absence of Mollie Longimore, and gave the order to "lie on your oars." At his request Susie did the same.

"Are you tired, girls?" asked Prince.

"Not one bit!" protested Kitty, in the Undine.

"We don't have to use any strength at all," said another.

"Can't we have a race?" asked Susie Thaxter.

"No; not on any account," replied Prince, decidedly. "By and by, when you have practised a great deal, and your muscles are a little hardened, we will do a little mild racing."

"There won't be any fun, if we can't race," pouted Kitty.

"I think there will be plenty of fun; but we shall have a race when you are in condition for it. You might do yourself more harm in one hour than you could recover from in a year, if you exercise too violently. For the present, you must pull no faster than the time I have given you. Now we will show off what you can do to the people on shore."

The rowers gave way again, and the Undine was instructed to follow the Dorcas. Prince led the way to a considerable distance below the boat-builder's pier, and then took a course back, which led the boats as near the shore as the depth of the water would permit. The girls, feeling now that they were on exhibition, threw back their shoulders, and did their best. The instructor counted the time loud enough for both crews to hear him, till the rowers in both boats were pulling precisely the same stroke. Their speed did not vary a particle, and the eight oars all dipped at precisely the same instant. As they passed close to the shore, and the pier where the other members of the club and the spectators were assembled, they were greeted with hearty applause.

"Ready to toss—toss!" said Prince, when the boats were abreast of the pier.

The eight oars were elevated to a perpendicular, as though they had all been parts of the same machine, the boats still shooting ahead under the impetus given them before. This was the complimentary salute with which a boat acknowleges a civility.

"Let fall! Give way!" continued Prince; and the rowing was resumed without a break in the time, calling from the spectators a renewed expression of approbation.

The boats circled around, and again passed the spectators, tossing the oars as before, in reply to the applause which greeted them. Prince then stopped the Dorcas, and directed the Undine to take a position abreast, and on the starboard side of her. Side by side, they passed the spectators, a third time, the ends of the oars almost touching, so careful was the steering. Again the fair rowers tossed their oars, in reply to the demonstrations on shore.

"Are you tired yet?" asked Prince, when they had been out an hour and a half.

No one was tired even in the slightest degree,

but the instructor deemed it prudent to return to the shore, where the two clubs were greeted with the warmest expressions of delight and admiration. Dr. Darling expressed the pleasure he felt in seeing the business conducted so well, and declared that the girls would be vastly benefited by the exercise thus prudently managed. The fresh air was good for them, and there was no danger at present of over-exertion.

"But such gentle rowing will soon become very tame to them," added the doctor.

"I suppose so, sir. But when they have more boats, they can perform all sorts of manœuvers, which will give them plenty of variety," replied Prince.

"You have two boats now, and one building?"

"Yes sir. Don John is building one besides, on his own account. I suppose the girls will not be satisfied till they have a boat for each of the five clubs."

"I wish they had them, for I think they need this exercise in the open air. Don't let them overdo it, on any account."

"I will not—if I can help it; but I suppose

my services will not be much longer required," added Prince, as he walked into the shop with the doctor.

"You are building a boat on your own account, Don John, I am told," said Dr. Darling.

"Yes, sir. I think there will be a demand for row-boats this season," replied the builder.

"It certainly looks like it now," laughed the doctor. "Do you intend to sell her?"

"Yes, sir — of course."

"I will take her, at the price named for the other, for the Dorcas Club. Let me see, Prince. What are the names of the clubs that have no boats?"

"The Fairy and the Psyche."

"Call this one the Psyche."

"Very well, sir."

Prince reported what Dr. Darling had done to the members of the club; and certainly the prospect was as bright as they could wish. The next afternoon the Psyche Club received its first lesson, the Lily Club using the Undine at the same time. On Saturday the Fairy Club took its turn; and when the week ended, all the clubs were able to pull a boat, though all of them still had a great deal to learn.

By this time Don John had the frames of the two boats set up, and all hands worked early and late upon them. Prince was quite as enthusiastic as any of the girls, and only regretted that Mollie Longimore could not take part in the sports; and his regret was shared by Minnie and Nellie. He continued to do all he could for the afflicted family, and called upon them three times a day. After the rowing was finished on Saturday, he found Minnie and Nellie at the cashier's house. Mollie and her mother had become in some degree reconciled to the altered circumstances; and, though they had not ceased to mourn him whom they believed to be no more, they were calm and composed.

"I am sorry you gave that white envelope to your father, Mollie," said Minnie, who had been waiting for a fit time to open this subject, and to return the money it had contained.

"I did not give it to him," replied Mollie.

"You did not?"

"I told you I could not; and I did not. I am so glad now that I did not!"

"But you gave it back to me sealed," added Minnie, greatly astonished.

"I didn't mind whether it was sealed or not.

But my father did not see it, or know anything about it."

" But every envelope contained money — every one of them."

" Mine had no money in it, I am sure," persisted Mollie. " I didn't like to carry the envelope and circular into the house, for fear some one might see them. I gave it for Prince to keep for me — didn't I, Prince ? "

" You did," replied he, rather puzzled to determine how he should get out of the scrape.

" Did you seal it?" asked Minnie.

" Why should he seal it when there was nothing in it ? "

" But every envelope contained money."

" Then Prince put the money into mine," said Mollie, blushing.

After some attempts to evade the issue, he was obliged to confess that he had put a ten-dollar bill into the envelope before he gave it back to Mollie. Minnie and Nellie both insisted upon returning it. Mollie would not take the money; and in the end Prince was forced to accept it; but when he put it into his pocket, he mentally determined that every cent of it should be spent for the benefit of the Longimores.

CHAPTER XII.

THE SOLITARY OARSMAN.

MONDAY, the first day of vacation, was a busy day with "Professor" Willingood, for each of the clubs was to have the use of one of the boats for two hours. The Dorcas and the Lily Clubs were to have their turn in the forenoon; and Prince took his place in the former for the first hour; but Carrie West, of the Psyche, acted as leader in the Dorcas, in the absence of Mollie Longimore.

"I told you the other day that there were several things more for you to learn," said the professor, when the boats were under way, and some distance from the land.

"I thought we had learned out," laughed Minnie. "We can row, and make the boat go. What more is there to do?"

"Do you see those two yachts, anchored close

together?" asked Prince, pointing to the Maud and the Sea Foam, which were lying within ten feet of each other.

"I see them."

"Suppose, in order to avoid being run down by a steamer, it suddenly became necessary for the Dorcas to pass between them."

"It would be simply impossible to row through such a narrow place," replied Minnie. "We should break our oars."

"Not at all."

"We could toss oars," suggested Nellie Patterdale.

"And if the wind were blowing pretty fresh, the blades of the oars would act as so many small sails, and might carry the boat against one of the yachts, or get you afoul of her rigging. It might be done; but it is not the best way. Before we go any farther, we will pass through that narrow place. When Carrie West gives the order, 'Ready to trail—trail!' at the last word, you will each throw the loom of the oar out of the rowlock, holding on at the handle. It must be done, of course, when the boat is under full headway. The motion of the boat

will bring all the blades of the oars alongside.
As soon as you are through the narrow place,
the order will be given, 'Ship your oars,' and
you will place the loom in the rowlock again.
Now we will try it. Give the word, Carrie,
'Ready to trail.'"

"Ready to trail!" repeated the leader.
"Trail!"

The oars were permitted to come alongside,
and held in this position, though some boats
have trail-lines attached to the oars and the
gunwale, so that the whole may be released.

"Very well, young ladies," said the professor,
as they insisted upon calling him. "Now when
you ship your oars, you must be careful not to
catch a crab."

"I know what that is," said Eva Doane.

"I am glad you do; but there is a difference
of opinion in regard to it," added Prince.
"Some say it is catching the oar in the water,
when gathering up for the stroke; and others,
that it is missing the stroke, or 'rowing dry,' so
that the rower is pitched over backwards. Now
haul your oars well in, and lift the blade out
of the water when you throw it into the row-

lock. Don't let it touch the water again till the order comes to 'give way.' Now try it, Carrie."

"Ship your oars!"

They were handled as in tossing; and, being proficient in this exercise, the new movement came very easily.

"Give way!" added Carrie; and the rowing was resumed as though there had been no break in it.

The operation of trailing was repeated several times before Prince would permit the boat to pass between the two yachts, the crews of which were on board, getting them ready for a cruise down the bay. The yachtmen watched the movements of the Dorcas and the Undine with no little interest and admiration; and when the former passed between their yachts, all hands gave three rousing cheers.

"Ready to toss! Toss!" said Carrie, prompted by Prince; and all the oars went up, in response to the command.

"Is there anything more to learn, Professor Willingood?" inquired Minnie.

"Plenty more, Miss President," answered

Prince. "Suppose a steamer should shoot out into the path of the boat, so that, if you did not stop the Dorcas, in going two or three times her length you would smash the steamer, or be smashed yourself, what would you do? That's the conundrum."

"Stop rowing and back water, of course," said Eva Doane.

"Just so but, —

> "'In colleges and halls, in ancient times,
>   There dwelt a sage called Discipline.'

It is rather a startling thing to find yourself in the path of a steamboat, for steamers have an ugly habit of smashing small boats like pipe-stems; and without discipline some might back, and others pull, and whirl the boat around, instead of getting out of the way. We will learn to do the thing properly, as they did it in colleges and halls in ancient days. The word is, 'Oars!' because no long speeches should be made when the boat is in danger."

"But that is the same order as when you lie upon the oars," Minnie objected.

"Very true; and that is precisely what you will do — lie upon your oars. The second order is, 'Hold water;' when you will drop the oars into the brine, just as in pulling the stroke. You must hold the handles firmly for the resistance may be so great as to throw you off your seats. Now go ahead again and we will try it."

"Give way," said the leader; and the girls pulled till the Dorcas was under full headway.

"Now is your time, Carrie," added Prince.

"Oars!" shouted Carrie, sharply.

Instantly every rower was lying on her oars, with the flat of the blade just above the water.

"Hold water!" added the leader, an instant later.

The girls turned the oars, and dropped them into the water. In a few moments the progress of the Dorcas was checked, and she lay motionless.

"Very well, indeed," said the instructor. "But it is often necessary to do something more than merely "hold water,' and the order, 'Stern, all!' is given, at which you must all row backwards or back water."

"We can do that," added Minnie.

"I know you can; but you need practice;

otherwise, an order quickly given may throw
you into confusion, at a time when you have
not a moment to spare. Now try it, Carrie.
Go ahead, hold water, and then back her."

"Give way!" said the leader; and the Dorcas darted off.

"I want you to notice how quickly you can
check her headway," continued Prince.

" Oars!" added the leader, at the right moment.
" Hold water! Stern, all!"

It was a failure, for in backing water the
rowers lost the stroke. Ruth was hit in the
back by the handle of Eva's oar, and all of
them were thrown into confusion.

"I thought you said you could do that,"
laughed Prince.

"Carrie gave the orders too rapidly," pleaded
Minnie.

"Not too rapidly," said the instructor. "If
there is danger ahead, you can't stop to dream
about it; you must act. Now, you must keep
doing it till the movement will execute itself,
for it is the most important one I have given
you. You will often be required to do it in
emergencies. When we have the four boats out,

you will be in constant peril of running into each other, if you don't know how to handle your boats properly."

Carrie started the boat again, and repeated the orders as before; but the club again failed to hit the back stroke together. The next time, it was done more slowly and with better success. The manœuvre was executed a dozen times before Prince was satisfied with it. As the first hour had expired, the Dorcas headed for the shore, in order to transfer the professor to the Undine, to whose crew he was to give the same lessons.

" In bow !" said Carrie, prompted by Prince, as the boat approached the landing-place.

Nellie Patterdale, who pulled the bow oar, unshipped it, and repaired to the four-sheets, with the light boat-hook in her hand, in readiness to fend off, or fasten to the pier.

" Way enough," added the leader; whereat the three remaining rowers tossed their oars, and then boated, or, in other words, deposited them in the boat by the gunwale, where they belonged.

The Dorcas lost her headway just as the bow

came up to the pier; but Prince had indicated to Carrie when to give the order.

"We hit it just right," said Nellie, as she hooked into the pier, and drew the boat alongside it.

"You must be very careful indeed, when you make a landing, to estimate the distance correctly," added the professor.

"I know the distance now," replied Carrie; "and I am sure I can hit it right every time."

"Don't be too sure," laughed Prince, shaking his head; "for it will hardly be twice the same. If the wind is blowing strong off shore, it will be less; if on shore, more. You must make the proper allowance every time; but you had better make too great rather than too small an allowance. It is safer to fall short of the pier, than to run into it, and smash your boat. Here comes the Undine; let us see how she does it."

She did it badly, for Kate Bilder made too little allowance for the headway of the boat, and if Prince had not caught the bow, she would have driven her stem into the pier. The professor took his place in the Undine, and went over the same ground as in the Dorcas. Before noon he had finished the lesson, and then both clubs practiced in making the pier. While they did so, Prince stood on the wharf, with a boat-hook in his hand, to prevent any accident; but the leaders were so careful that the boats fell short every time. This was a mistake on the safe side, and the instructor was satisfied to leave the matter where it was. The lessons for the forenoon were finished, the boats secured, and all hands went home to dinner. At two o'clock the rowing was resumed by the Undine and Psyche Clubs, and the professor repeated his instructions till they had become rather monotonous to him. At four o'clock, he went over the old story with the Fairy Club, in the Undine, the Dorcas Club using the other boat.

"Hullo!"

The shout came from a small boat, pulled by one man, directly ahead of the Psyche. Carrie West was putting her knowledge to a practical test, steering the boat towards the craft before her, intending to "hold water," and "back her," in season to avoid a collision. The lonely oarsman seemed to fear a catastrophe, and had thrown up a warning note; but the intrepid leader of the Psyche brought her to a dead stand not more than half a boat's length from him.

"Hullo!" yelled the man, as the Psyche stopped; "are you go'n to run into me?"

"I hadn't the least idea of doing so, sir," replied Carrie.

"That's rather a close shave," added the solitary rower, shaking his head.

"We can do it nineteen times more, without touching you," laughed the leader.

"I'd ruther you don't try it again. You'll break the bow of that pretty boat all to flinders, if you cut so clost," added the stranger.

"No danger, sir."

"But it makes my nerves rather shakey. I've got as many nerves as a lady."

"We will not go near you again, then," added Carrie.

"I'm ruther glad you fetched up so clost, for I want to see you."

"See me!" exclaimed the leader, merrily.

"Well, no; not exactly the gal, but the feller with you.— Be you J. Prince Willingood? "

" That's my name."

" He's the professor," chuckled Carrie.

" I s'pose so," added the lonely rowist, who did not indulge in a smile, much less a laugh, but looked as solemn as an owl. " I want to see the professor. I want to talk with him."

" I'm engaged just now," replied Prince.

" Engaged to all them gals?" queried the man, gloomily.

" We release you from the engagement," laughed Carrie.

" I will be at Don John's boat-house in a few minutes," added Prince. " I will see you there."

" That's half a mile off, and I ain't so fond of rowing as them gals. I want to see you very bad."

" How bad? "

" Bad enough to do almost anything."

" Who is he, Prince? " asked one of the girls.

" It's Simon Potter, I think," replied Prince.

" That's my name; and I live in the woods down to Northport," added the man, whose hearing was excellent, though he seemed to be somewhat advanced in years. If you git into my boat, I'll pull you up to the boat-shop while we're talkin'."

"We can return without you, professor," said Carrie.

"You won't break the wharf down when you land — will you?"

"I will try not to do so," replied Carrie.

"Because we shall want it this season, and don't wish to have it smashed."

"I will be careful."

. "Very well. I will see what this worthy gentleman desires. Pull, starboard; back, port oars."

The Undine swung around, so that Prince could step into the boat of the solitary oarsman. As he seated himself in the stern, the club gave way again, and was soon out of hailing distance.

"You don't know me much, Prince," said Simon Potter.

"Not much."

The lonely rower had the reputation of being a strange man, and his looks were fully up to his reputation. He was short in stature, being not more than five feet four in height. His hair was always cut short, and what there was of it was of a yellowish-white; but his beard, of the same color, reached nearly down to his waist. He always wore coarse gray pants, very large and bagging, and a short blue frock, reaching to his hips, over whatever other garments he had on. Winter and summer, his fashion was always the same. His hat — when he wore any — was an ordinary "stove-pipe," at least so far as the brim was concerned; but he had cut away the crown, and rolled it up into the shape of a cone. Certainly it was a "shocking bad hat," and those who saw it upon his head immediately concluded that Simon Potter was a crazy man If he walked through the streets of the city, every boy stopped and turned round to look at him as a curiosity.

If the solitary rower was not crazy, he was eccentric. The tradition in regard to him was that he had graduated at Bowdoin College, studied medicine, and established himself in practice. He was married; but being a singular man, his wife could not live with him, and de-

16

serted him. This misfortune seemed to disgust him with civilization and society. In order to get away from everybody, he "camped out" for a summer on the lonely Northport shore. Then he bought a considerable tract of land, and built a small house and barn upon it, where he lived entirely alone. He cultivated ground enough to afford him all the vegetables he wanted, and to enable him to keep a cow. If anybody called to see him, he was not at home, for he concealed himself in the woods, when he saw visitors approaching. Two or three times a year, he went to the city to purchase supplies and collect his interest, for he had money invested there.

"Nobody knows me much," said Simon Potter. "I don't want to know folks much. I keep out of the way."

"Why do you keep out of the way?" asked Prince.

"Because it suits me best. I don't like folks any better'n folks like me. We don't agree; and I'm willin' to let them alone, if they'll let me alone."

"I have heard it said that you were a doctor."

"I ain't no doctor now. I used to be, but I ain't now, and don't mean to be agin. I got tired o' livin' when I wan't more'n thirty years old. I've been ready to die ever since; I'm only waitin' for my time to come. I don't trouble nobody, and nobody troubles me — except peddlers and lightnin'-rod men."

"You must be very lonely."

"No, I ain't. I don't want no company, and never have none. How deep do you suppose the water is down here?" said the strange man, resting on his oars, and looking into the water.

"I don't know; fifty feet, perhaps," replied Prince.

"I s'pose you knew Mr. Longimore?"

"Very well, indeed."

"Do you s'pose he's down there?" added Simon Potter, pointing impressively into the water.

"I'm afraid he is."

"Drowned?"

"Yes."

"He was a good man. He used to git my interest for me, and give it to me without laughin' at me, as other folks do. I'm sorry he's dead."

"He was a fine man."

"Yes he was. He never bothered me with questions I don't want to answer. He told me once that you were a good boy."

"I try to be."

"I want you to do some things for me. Will you? I'll pay you for it."

"I shall be glad to do anything I can for you," answered Prince, promptly.

"Now Mr. Longimore's gone, I want somebody to collect my interest for me, and bring it to me, for I don't want to go to the city any more. Folks stare at me, and laugh at me. You can buy some things for me, when I want 'em. I'll pay you well for all you do."

"I will do anything of this kind you wish."

"Thank ye, Prince;" and Simon Potter suddenly relapsed into a fit of deep musing, during which he gazed intently into the water.

"When shall I collect your interest, Dr. Potter?" asked the young man, when he was tired of the silence.

"Don't call me doctor. I'm no doctor now."

"Excuse me — Mr. Potter."

"Nor mister, nuther. Call me Simon Potter.

Do you suppose Mr. Longimore has gone to heaven, Prince?"

"He was a Christian man, and I have no doubt of it."

"If he ain't dead?"

"Well, no; not if he is alive."

"Folks think he's gone to heaven, — don't they?"

"I don't know what they think. Probably those who believe he stole the bonds don't think so."

"How old are you, Prince?" asked Simon Potter, looking him earnestly in the face.

"Seventeen."

"Have you come to years of discretion yet?"

"I think I have," laughed Prince.

"Some boys don't never come to years of discretion, added the strange man, solemnly.

"Are you afraid to trust me with your interest money, Mr. Potter?"

"Simon Potter is my name. I shall soon be in the Potter's Field."

The words sounded like a grim joke; but the speaker did not smile. He never smiled.

"I hope not," added Prince.

"Don't wish me ill. I ain't afraid to trust you with my interest money. It's due the first day of July. The cashier used to have it ready for me the next day. Do you s'pose Mr. Longimore is dead?"

"His wife and daughter think so; and I have no reason to doubt it," answered Prince.

"His folks feel bad — don't they?"

"Very badly."

"I'm sorry for 'em, for Mr. Longimore was a good man. I'm sorry they think he is dead, I mean."

"Don't you think he was drowned?" asked Prince, perplexed by the odd speech of his companion.

"I love the cashier. He's the only man on the airth I care for. He don't laugh at me."

"But isn't he drowned?" demanded Prince.

"The water's fifty feet deep here, you say. If you tell anybody what I say, Prince, except them I tell you to tell, those who want to know more about it will find my body at the bottom of the bay, fifty feet down."

"What do you mean, sir?"

"If you say one word more'n I tell you to, you'll wrong me, and you'll wrong —"

"Whom?" asked Prince, when the old man paused.

"Mr. Longimore!"

Prince was thoroughly excited now.

CHAPTER XIII.

MOTHER AND DAUGHTER.

"DO you really mean that Mr. Longimore is alive?" asked Prince of his eccentric companion.

"I hope I hain't made no mistake in tellin' you," replied Simon Potter, doubtfully.

"You have not made a mistake; that is—"

Prince stopped there, for it suddenly occurred to him that he could not be a party to the concealment of one charged with robbing the bank of forty thousand dollars in bonds.

"That is!" repeated the strange man. "I see! I ain't no doctor, but I can read your thoughts. Mr. Longimore won't be sent to jail; he'll die fust. I won't be the cause of sendin' him to jail; I'll die fust. Now, Prince, let me tell you jest how it'll all work. You'll go up to the city, tell the president of the bank,

PRINCE AND THE SOLITARY OAKSMAN.   Page 243.

or the deputy sheriff, or some one else, that Mr.
Longimore is alive, and that Simon Potter knows
something about him. The sheriff comes down
to Northport to look after me. He don't find me.
Where am I? A cold body, fifty feet under
water. I can't tell nothin' then — can I?"

"I should say not," replied Prince, breathless
with interest.

"He can't git even a hint out of me; but
the sheriff will start from my place to look after
the cashier. Where is he? A cold body, fifty
feet under water! He won't do the bank officers
no good then."

"But where is Mr. Longimore?"

"I hain't told you."

"You have as good as told me he is alive,"

"Then his life and mine is in your hands,"
replied Simon Potter. "He couldn't stand it
no longer; and sumthin' had to be done. He
fixed on you to do it."

"What can I do? I'm only a boy," pleaded
Prince, awed by the awful responsibility imposed
upon him.

"Only tell his wife and the oldest darter that
he ain't dead. Nothin' more."

"But how can I know anything about him, and keep still, when he is charged with robbing the bank?" added Prince.

"He is as innocent as you are of stealing the bonds," protested Simon Potter, so excited that he dropped the illiterate style of speaking, which he had adopted from the first, apparently to do away with the impression that he might be a doctor.

"Innocent!" exclaimed the young man.

"He is innocent; but he may never be able to prove his innocence."

"Where are the bonds, then?"

"I cannot answer you. Will you keep the poor man's secret? Will you save him from death? Answer me at once."

"Is it right for me to keep such a secret?"

"Settle that for yourself. I am not the keeper of your conscience. It is right for me to keep it, for I know he is innocent."

"I am afraid to promise," replied Prince, sadly bewildered by the difficulty of the situation.

"I respect your scruples, Prince; but Mr. Longimore's life is in your hands. His hope is in you. For more reasons than I am permitted to name now, he has chosen you to help him.

If you disappoint him, he has nothing to hope for in this world."

"But I cannot promise to conceal a crime. I have no right to do it," protested Prince.

"I don't wish you to conceal a crime. There has been no crime to conceal. I am not desperately wicked and given over to sin and iniquity, any more than yourself, young man," added Simon Potter. "I would no more conceal a crime than you would. That is not the point."

"What is the point, then?" asked Prince, deeply interested.

"'There comes them gals agin," said the strange man, suddenly resuming his usual dialect, and putting on the hat with the conic crown. "Gals has ears."

But the Undine only shot past the solitary rower, and was soon out of hearing.

"Them gals will want to know what my business was with you," said Simon Potter, with a rather troubled expression, as he took off the conic hat, and placed it on the thwart by his side.

"You wished me to collect your interest for

you. You do not object to my saying as much as that to them if asked — do you? "

" No, I don't."

" It will be no more than the truth."

" It is only a small part of the truth ; and half the truth is sometimes as much a lie as a deliberate falsehood. You mean to be honest, Prince ; but don't cheat yourself. Don't believe you are honest when you are not. Thieves, swindlers, and cheats persuade themselves that they are honest. Instead of telling half the truth, say to the girls that the matter does not concern them. That's honest."

" I don't think it is a lie to tell as much of the truth as I think proper, when the truth does not concern those asking the questions," replied Prince, who had some very clear ideas of his own on this subject, whether they were right or wrong.

" You may judge for yourself on that point," added Simon Potter. " Men and women are full of lies and deceit. They cheat and defraud each other. But this is not the question now."

" You began to tell me what the point was."

" You are not asked to conceal a crime, or to

favor the escape of a criminal. Mr. Longimore is not a thief or a robber, whatever the people of the city may think.

"I am very glad to hear you say so."

"But you don't believe what I say."

"I certainly desire to believe it."

"That is all I ask. Now to the point. The cashier is practically charged with a crime. If he could be found, he would be arrested and thrown into jail. This would break his heart, which would be the same thing as breaking his neck. The bonds are gone ; the cashier is gone. These two things would convict him, under the circumstances. The story he has to tell would not be believed, for the only witness he has will lie, will perjure himself, will send him to the penitentiary for life, in order to enable the perjurer to make a hundred dollars."

" Who is the witness ? "

"I cannot tell you ; but I have told you the exact truth. I would not tell a lie to save my neck from the gallows, or my body from a damp grave fifty feet under the cold waters of the bay. I ask of you only two things."

" What are they ? "

"First, that you will tell Mrs. Longimore her husband is alive."

"I will do that with the greatest pleasure."

"But you must not mention my name."

"Will she believe me?

"She will; or, if she will not, she shall not remain twenty-four hours in doubt."

"Where is Mr. Longimore?" asked Prince, shaking himself to make sure that he was not dreaming.

"I will not tell you yet."

"Well, what is the other thing I am to do?"

"You are to see Mr. Longimore, and satisfy yourself of the truth of what I said, before you speak to any living soul, except the cashier's wife and daughter."

"Certainly I will do that. But when may I see him?"

"This night."

"I promise, then, to keep the secret till I have seen him."

"Very well; but you must remember that any treachery on your part will cost him his life."

"I am not capable of treachery, Simon Potter. I have tried to believe that Mr. Longimore was guilty of no crime ; and until I have seen him — if I am indeed to see him — nothing shall induce me to betray him. I could not do that. Where is he? "

" At my house in the woods. That is all I can tell you now. You must come to-night ; you must come alone. No one must see you. I will meet you at the mouth of Little River, at any hour you say."

Prince actually trembled when he realized the nature of the adventure he was to engage in ; but he was a plucky boy ; and he believed the strange inhabitant of the Northport wood was honest and sincere, high-toned and high-minded. He considered the situation for a moment before he made any reply. Whatever he did, he must do without the knowledge of Fox Bushwell, or any other person.

" I will be at the mouth of Little River about half past ten to-night," said he, "or as near that time as I can. It may be half an hour earlier, or half an hour later."

" It will not harm me to wait. I am used

to the night and the darkness, the cold and the storm," added Simon Potter. "As soon as you can, tell the poor wife that her husband lives."

" I will; I only fear that she will not believe me, because I cannot tell her any more," replied Prince.

" She shall believe you."

Simon Potter drew in one of his oars, and, raising his short blue frock, he took from one of his pockets a dirty slip of paper, which he handed to his companion.

" What is that?"

" It is a message in writing from the husband to his wife. I dared not speak of it before. If it should be found, all will be lost. There is death to the cashier in that note, if it should be seen by any one but his wife and the oldest daughter. Do you understand? Beware, young man!"

Prince thought the solitary oarsman was becoming a little melodramatic, and he could not help asking himself whether the business in which he was engaged was not some trick, some fancy of a disordered brain. As he was

thinking, he opened the unsealed note in his
hand. It was certainly the writing of the cashier, with which the young man was quite
familiar. He read it, and then carefully placed
the paper in his wallet. The boat in which he
sat was still far from the shop of Don John
for Simon had hardly rowed at all during the
conversation.

"I guess it's all fixed now," said the strange
man, with the nearest appearance to a smile
which Prince had yet seen upon his face; and
with this remark he resumed his old tone and
his usual dialect.

"If you will land me on the beach here, I
will not trouble you to pull up to the boat-
shop, added Prince, glancing at the shore, near
which Simon had kept his boat, to avoid meeting other craft.

"That'll be a good deal better'n goin' up to
the shop, and givin' them that's there sumthin'
to talk about," added the oarsman, as, with a
few vigorous strokes, he drove his craft far up
on the beach.

"I can walk up in a few moments."

"Now, remember, young man, that the life

17

of one that never did nothin' wrong to no one is in your hands," said Simon Potter, in a low tone.

" Tell him he can trust me, and that I will do all that a mortal can do to help him."

Prince shoved the old man's boat back into the deep water, and then hastened up to the boat-shop, where he arrived at six o'clock, just as the Dorcas and the Undine came in. He assisted in housing the boats, and the girls were so full of enthusiasm in regard to the excursion, that he thought he should be asked no questions about his relations with the strange man of the Northport woods, but he was mistaken.

" What in the world did that old man with the conic section on his head want of you, Professor Willingood?" asked Carrie West.

" He wanted me to do some business for him. Strange as he is, that old man owns land and has money invested in the city."

" What does he wear that awful hat for?"

" Why do you wear such a funny hat?"

" Because it is the fashion."

" Well, that hat is Simon Potter's fashion. He is a fashion unto himself. But I must go

home ;" and Prince ran away with more abrupt-
ness than he often dared to use with the girls.

He went home and ate his supper, which was
all ready when he arrived. It was not a bad
supper, for Fox Bushwell had provided much
better for the table since the scene with his
ward. But Prince, hungry as he was, thought
less of his supper than usual that evening. Half
a dozen times while he was eating, he put his
hand into his pocket to assure himself of the
safety of the wallet containing that little slip of
paper. What a sensation that note would make
if its contents were known to the people of the
city! If the editor of the newspaper could get
hold of it, he would doubtless issue an extra, to
inform his patrons of the astounding intelligence
it revealed.

Prince kept as calm as he could ; but as soon
as his meal was finished, he hastened to the
house of the cashier. The time was opportune,
for the younger children had all been sent to
bed, and Mrs. Longimore and Mollie were alone
in the sitting-room.

"Anything for me to do, Mrs. Longimore?"
asked Prince, with more cheerfulness than he

had dared to exhibit since the departure of the cashier.

"Nothing at all, Prince. You are very kind to take so much care of us," replied Mrs. Longimore.

"I should be ashamed of myself if I did any less. If you only knew how happy it makes me to help you, you would let me do more. It is vacation this week, and I have plenty of time."

"I heard you were very busy teaching the girls how to row."

"I have been; but they can all row pretty well now, and, like Othello, my occupation's gone."

"Minnie and Nellie were here this afternoon," continued Mrs. Longimore. "They let me have another hundred dollars, though I do not need it. I have used but little of the first money they gave me. I protested against taking it; but they said I must. They want Mollie to go back to school next Monday."

"I hope she will do so. She will graduate next year, and it will be a pity for her not to have her diploma."

"I cannot go and leave mother to do all the work," said Mollie.

"There is no more work than before," added the mother, who evidently favored the idea.

"But I cannot go. I don't think I ought to associate with the other girls now," replied Mollie, as the tears started in her eyes.

"The girls don't think so," interposed Prince. "You were chosen leader of the Dorcas Club."

"The girls are very kind. They have treated me ever so much better than I deserve."

"I am sure they have not," protested Prince, earnestly. "They hope you will be in the boat some time this week, and learn your part as leader."

"O, no; I cannot do that."

"Why not?"

"My poor father!" sobbed Mollie.

"She don't feel like doing anything," added Mrs. Longimore, wiping away her own tears.

"While we are living on charity, I cannot think of joining any boat club," said Mollie. "I can't help thinking of poor father every hour, and almost every minute of the day. If he had died at home—"

"Perhaps he is not dead," suggested Prince, who hardly dared to tell his good news at once. "Indeed, I believe he is not dead."

"If he is not dead, I am afraid he is worse than dead," added the poor wife. "I would rather he were buried in the deep waters of the bay, than feel all my life that he is a felon."

"You look on the dark side of the case, Mrs. Longimore. Perhaps he is neither dead nor a felon."

"If he is alive I am afraid he took the bonds."

"Perhaps not."

"I will not believe poor father is guilty of a crime," added Mollie, so grieved that Prince dared not say what he had to say.

"Let us not talk about it. It is a terrible mystery which we cannot fathom," interposed the wife.

"But I am almost sure we shall learn something about the matter before long," continued Prince, a little more decidedly, as he gradually felt his way to the great revelation he had to make.

"What do you mean, Prince?" demanded Mrs. Longimore.

Mollie wiped away her tears, and gazed stead-fastly at the young man.

"Of course I can't tell," added Prince.

"Have the bank people obtained any news, or any clew?"

"No," replied Prince, emphatically. "I would not have any of them know what I have said for all the world."

"What have you said?"

"I only said I was almost sure we should hear something from Mr. Longimore before long."

"Why don't you explain what you mean?" demanded Mrs. Longimore with intense emotion.

"If you know that he is dead, Prince, do not conceal it from us. We can bear anything now," added Mollie.

"I don't believe he is dead, and I have reason to think he is innocent of anything wrong."

"Tell us what you know, Prince. You don't know what agony you are causing me," pleaded the stricken wife. "You have something to tell us—I know you have."

"I have; but before I say a single word, I must caution you not to repeat one word I say, or even hint at it."

"Then there is something wrong."

"I think not; at least, I hope not."

"You hope not?"

"I believe not; but I don't know much about it. You must keep still, at least for a day or two, or until you or I know more about it."

"Certainly we can do nothing to injure poor father, if he is still living," said Mollie, wrought up to the highest pitch of anxiety.

"Mr. Longimore *is* still alive," added Prince.

"Where is he?" gasped the wife.

"O, Prince!" groaned Mollie.

"I don't know that I ought to tell even you where he is; but I shall see him to-night," replied Prince in a whisper, as he glanced at the windows.

"Can it be true?"

"You may depend upon it," added the messenger of Simon Potter, as he took from his wallet the dirty slip of paper. "Be calm, now; for if we make the slightest mistake, Mr. Longimore may not long be alive."

With a struggle the mother and daughter, awed by these fearful words, regained in some degree their self-possession.

THE BRIEF NOTE WAS GIVEN TO MRS. LONGIMORE.   Page 265.

"We must all be very prudent," continued Prince. "Are you calm enough to read a line from him?"

"O, yes! Give it to me!"

The brief note was given to Mrs. Longimore, and panting with emotion, she read it to herself.

"What is it, mother? Read it!" cried Mollie.

Mrs. Longimore, with faltering utterance, read the note, as follows:—

"MY DEAR WIFE AND CHILDREN: I am still alive, but I am suffering what no words can tell. I am guilty of no crime, though everything is against me. Help me, by your silence, to prove my innocence. I could not live another day without telling you I am not a felon. Send Prince to me, for he may be able to save me.

R. L."

The mother and daughter wept together; and for some time Prince respected their silence, hardly able to restrain his own tears.

"You are satisfied now—are you?" he asked, at last.

"I am, Prince; it seems like a dream," replied the poor wife.

"That's father's writing, certainly," added Mollie, as she took the slip of paper from her mother.

"All that I have said is true to the letter," said Prince.

"But where is he?"

"He is not three miles from here."

"And you are to see him to-night?"

"I am."

"Can't I see him? May I not go with you?"

"I must do just as I was told to do. I must go alone. But you shall hear from him again in the morning. I will not sleep till I tell you all I know," replied the young man, glancing at the clock.

"If he is innocent, why did he go away?" asked Mrs. Longimore.

"I don't know; I cannot explain it. Perhaps he lost the bonds; perhaps some one stole them. Probably he went off on account of the loss of the bonds; but he says he is innocent, and we must take his word for it till we know to the contrary. He may have made some mistake, without meaning to do wrong, and was afraid to meet the directors of the bank."

"If he is not guilty of a crime, I don't care for anything else," added Mrs. Longimore.

"I am going now. If I get back before day-light, shall I come here?"

"Yes. Ring the bell; I shall hear it," replied the poor lady.

Prince went home.

CHAPTER XIV.

IN THE GLOOM OF THE NIGHT.

POSSIBLY Prince Willingood's standard in regard to deception was not so high as that of Simon Potter, and he made a distinction between telling all he knew and wilfully deceiving any one. He did not tell Fox Bushwell what he had done that day, nor what he intended to do that night; and the old man had no suspicion that any unusual events were in progress. If Fox Bushwell got his eye on a dollar which might possibly be raked into his coffers, he paid but little heed to anything else. He kept his gaze fixed on that dollar until it was hidden in his own pocket. Since the fire he had been very busy putting his new house in order, and looking after the insurance upon the one which was destroyed. The company was not ready to pay him. The officers asked him a great many questions in regard to the origin of the fire. They had inquired of Mrs. Pining and Prince in regard to this matter. Then they wanted to know something more in regard to the value of the property destroyed. Fox Bushwell had never insured any houses or furniture before, and he had taken out this policy only a month before the fire.

The insurance company did not say that anything was wrong, or even that they suspected anything was wrong. They only delayed payment, and asked questions — not very awkward questions, but such as caused Fox Bushwell to wonder what they were driving at. If they suspected any irregularity, why didn't they say so, and give him the opportunity to defend himself, and to show conclusively that the origin of the fire was a dense mystery, which no human being could find out?

He had gone to bed as usual that night, but rather later than his ordinary time — at half past ten, — had gone to sleep, and had been called by Prince. That was all he knew about it. Neither Mrs. Pining nor Prince contradicted his statement in any important particular.

Fox Bushwell was interested in this business matter, and he gave but little attention to anything else for the time being. In fact, it troubled him, though he did not say so. He had not slept well nights since the inquiry began; and when his ward came into the house, after his visit to the house of the Longimores, the old man was considerably exhausted; in fact, ready to sleep. At nine o'clock, Mrs. Pining retired; she always went to bed at that hour, whether she was sleepy or not. Fox Bushwell bolted the front door, and retreated to his room a few moments later.

Prince was wide awake, and, as may well be supposed, he was intensely excited in view of the night's work before him. He waited till he was satisfied that his uncle was asleep, or till he ought to have been asleep, and then went into the back-room. He did not like to go out, to be absent so long, leaving a door unfastened behind him, for he knew not what treasures the money-lender might have in the house. After looking over the ground, he decided to get out at one of the windows, which was so high that no one could easily get in at it from the outside, if he left it unfastened, though he knew how to get in himself, if he should happen to return in season to do so. He got out the window, and "hung off," dropping upon the grass beneath. The sash came down with a slam as he dropped, but it was so far from the sleepers in the house that they were not likely to hear it.

Walking on the grass, and stepping very carefully, he gained the street. The night was cloudy and dark, thus favoring his expedition. He hastened to the boat-shop of Don John, where he could obtain a small boat, which the owner allowed him to use whenever he wished. On the way he could not help thinking what he should say to his uncle in case his absence was discovered; but he did not worry himself in regard to such a contingency, for his uncle seldom questioned him as to where he had been, or what he had been doing. In the vicinity of the shop all was as still as a tomb. There was no light in Mrs. Ramsey's cottage; and the boat-builder, who was an early riser, was doubtless fast asleep, though it was only half past nine o'clock. Prince found the oars under the shop, and silently embarked on his gloomy voyage.

Though not a member of the Yacht Club, he was thoroughly experienced in the handling of boats, and knew the bay and harbor quite as well as the average of the boys of the city. On the high ground of the city were two spires whose outline could be seen on the sky, dark as the night was; and Prince knew that these two steeples, kept in range from the boat-shop, made a course that would carry the navigator clear of the trend of the coast projecting out into the bay north of the mouth of Little River.

Pulling out from the pier, he "brought the two spires into one," as nautical men express it. He was sorry no sail-boat was available, for a three-mile pull is not particularly pleasant, all alone in a dark night, even when one knows the course, and feels quite at home in the boat. But Prince kept thinking and kept rowing for an hour. He passed the headland, and then followed the shore towards the river. It could not have been ten minutes either way from the time he had appointed to be at the meeting-place, when he lay upon his oars, to listen for any sound which might indicate the presence of

Simon Potter, who, if there, could not have failed to hear the stroke of his oars.

" Hoo, hoo, hoo! " were the first sounds which saluted the waiting ears of the boatman.

It might be Simon Potter, or it might be a cat-owl.

" Hoo, hoo, hoo! " replied Prince; and Simon Potter might have thought it was the voice of his expected visitor or a cat-owl.

" Prince! " said a voice on the shore.

" Simon Potter! " replied the young man; and, resuming his oars, he soon beached his boat.

" You are on time," said the recluse of the Northport woods, as the visitor leaped upon the land.

" Yes, sir; everything worked well for me. My uncle went to bed earlier than he does sometimes, so that the coast was clear."

" Mr. Longimore is waiting for you in an agony of doubt. He feels that he has staked everything upon your judgment and fidelity," added Simon Potter.

" He has made no mistake. I only hope he will be able to show that he is innocent of any crime,"

18

replied Prince, as he fastened the painter of the boat to a tree.

"That is all that troubles him. The fact is, he can't prove anything. But follow me, and you shall see him very soon."

Simon Potter led the way through the woods, and in a few moments he arrived at his little cottage, which would have no more than satisfied the ambition of a thrifty day-laborer. Connected with it was a small barn, in which he kept his cow and pig. There was no light in the house; and Prince groped his way after his conductor, who led him to a chair.

"Sit down, Prince. We have no lights here, under the present circumstances. I will call him; and then I shall stay outside, to guard against any possible surprise."

"But where is Mr. —— "

"Don't speak his name," interposed Simon Potter. "Prudence costs nothing, and a miser can afford to be careful. You need not know where he is concealed, for the sheriff might come here a dozen times without suspecting his hiding-place."

The strange man left the room; and Prince

thought, from the sound of his footsteps, that he went in the direction of the barn. It was some time before the silence was again disturbed.

"Prince!" said a voice, trembling with fear or emotion.

"Here," replied the young man, rising from his chair; and the next moment his hand was grasped by one that seemed very cold and bony to him.

"I am not a felon," gasped the cashier, for of course it was he, though his name was not to be spoken, even in the solitude of the woods. "Will you believe me?"

The hand trembled, and the quiver of it seemed to be conveyed through the frame of the visitor.

"I am willing to believe it," replied Prince.

"But how are they — my wife and children?" whispered Mr. Longimore.

"They are well; but they have suffered more than I can tell."

"So have I, more than any one can tell. I have seen the newspaper, and I know that some people think that I committed suicide. I was tempted to do that. I intended to end the life

which was overshadowed and broken down by
a calamity for which I am not resposible. Simon
Potter saved me. He bade me live, at least
till I could learn whether my life was worth
saving," groaned Mr. Longimore, as he led
Prince to the only window of the room, at
which they seated themselves.

Accustomed now to the darkness, the young
man could see a dim outline of the cashier's
face. It was so white and so thin that the
visitor could easily have persuaded himself, if
he had been superstitious, that he was in com-
munion with one from another world. Mr.
Longimore took his hand again, as though the
warmth of the young blood carried heat to his
cold heart and his cold frame.

"Where is the boat in which you left the
city?" asked Prince, intent upon solving some
of the dark questions in the case which had
perplexed the gossips as well as the officers of
police.

"I don't know, Prince. Simon Potter took
care of it, and I know not whether he has
hidden, burned, or sunk it. I had something
else to think of, and I did not care. He will

tell you. I came here early on that Tuesday morning, a week ago, before even the sailors on the vessels in the harbor were stirring, for I kept close to the shore, where none could see me. But I was seeking only a grave. I desired only to send a message to my wife, that she and my children might not carry it rankling in their hearts, that I had died guilty of a crime. Simon Potter loved me, and has saved me so far."

"But if you had done nothing wrong, why did you leave the city?" asked Prince.

"Perhaps I was a coward. Now I believe that I was," sobbed the poor man. "The bonds were gone, and I was not brave enough to tell the directors that they were all destroyed."

"Destroyed?"

"Yes, destroyed; burned to ashes," groaned the cashier; and his companion could feel the tremor of his frame, as he clasped the hand he held more closely.

"How could they be burned?" asked Prince intensely excited.

"They were burned with your uncle's house."

"I don't understand it."

"I will tell you the whole story. It was for that I wished to see you," answered the cashier. "Do you know why I wished to see you rather than any one else?"

"I hope it was because you thought you could trust me."

"It was for that, certainly; but for another reason, also."

"What is it?"

"Because you live in the house of Fox Bushwell. He is your uncle, I know; but he is a hard man."

"I ought to know that as well as the next person," added Prince, heartily.

"But I am afraid he is not an honest man. God forgive me, if I wrong him! I would not speak ill of any one."

"I don't think you are very far from the truth."

"Do you think he could be guilty of any great crime?"

"I don't know about that; I shouldn't want to say. I'm afraid he would do almost anything for money. He loves it more than he loves his own soul, in spite of his preaching."

"I will tell you the whole story, Prince, and I hope you will be able to help me. My only reliance is upon you."

The cashier related all the incidents which had occurred upon that eventful Monday night, as they were detailed in a preceding chapter.

"My uncle took the wrong bundle of papers when he left the bank," said Prince, musing. "They were burned in the fire. But wouldn't the government replace the bonds, if it can be proved that they were burned?"

"Perhaps it would, if it could be proved beyond a doubt. I want to know if it can be proved."

"Certainly it can. Uncle Fox will help you."

"Will he? Do you know that he will?" asked Mr. Longimore, eagerly.

"I don't see how he can do anything else," added Prince.

"Has he told any one that the bonds were destroyed?"

"I don't know that he has," answered the young man, perplexed by the situation.

If Fox Bushwell knew that the bonds were destroyed, why had he not told the directors the truth ? Assuredly he did know it, for he and the cashier had searched for the papers after the fire, finding nothing but the empty brass kettle.

"Prince, I have had seven days to think of this terrible matter. I have blamed myself for not telling the whole truth that morning, instead of running away like a felon; but, after all, I think I have been wise, as men of the world are wise. I have consulted expediency rather than absolute justice. I have trusted to myself, rather than the simple truth, for safety. If I had staid in the city, I should have been arrested before dinner time. I should have been awaiting my trial at this moment in a prison."

"I suppose you did what you thought was best," added Prince.

"I was crazy with excitement when I found the bonds were gone; when I realized that they had been burned in the flames of your uncle's house, I could not think ; I was beside myself. I demanded the bonds of Fox Bushwell in the morning but he could only tell me they were burned; and I believed him then."

"Don't you believe him now ? " asked Prince.

"God forgive me if I wrong him! I don't

know whether or not they are destroyed. They
may be. Doubtless they are. I know not.
Will Fox Bushwell say they are burned? Will
he tell the whole truth?"

" Why not?"

" Why *has* he not told it?"

" I don't know; I don't understand it," said
the bewildered young man.

"As I read it in the newspaper, Fox Bushwell said I was rather wild in my manner; that
I gave him the bundle of papers he had left
at the bank, only saying I thought he might
want them. The — Your uncle says this was
all that passed between us," continued Mr. Longimore, gasping with emotion.

" Well, wasn't it all?"

" All? No. I demanded the bonds of him;
I was wild; I thrust my fist through the glass
to gain admission to the house. I was crazy
with the agony of the discovery that the bonds
were not in the bank vault. I demanded them
as I would one of my children if he had kid-
napped it. I shook my clinched fist in his face;
I grasped him by the throat; I told him I was
ruined, that my wife and children were ruined.

He told me, trembling like an aspen beneath my grasp, that the bonds were burned. Not one word does he say of all this when Mr. Doane and the directors asked him about the interview; only, that I gave him the papers, saying that he might want them, and then fled in an instant. If there had been a house very near, its inmates might have heard all I said. I was furious, for it was a matter of life or death to me; of what is better than life, or worse than death. Not one word did he say of what he knew to be the truth."

"Perhaps he was afraid to say anything for fear he might get into trouble himself," suggested Prince. "He is a timid man."

"Perhaps fear sealed his lips — I don't know. I would not wrong him. I have thought it all over a thousand times in my solitude. Night and day I have considered it. Through you, Prince, I must seek the truth. You are a good, brave boy; and you will help me?"

"I will, •with all the powers I have."

"Thank you, Prince. It is terrible to think of being branded as a felon, as I am. It is terrible to think of a cell in a prison; but it is

worse to think of my good name blighted, and
my poor family weeping over my living tomb!"

The cashier sobbed in bitterness of spirit, and
Prince sought to change the current of his
thought.

"Very likely my uncle was afraid to tell the
whole truth," said he.

"When was he questioned in regard to this
interview?"

"Not till late in the afternoon of the day you
left."

"Then he believed I could not come from my
watery grave in the bay to confront him,"
added the cashier, who seemed to be filled with
grave suspicions, though he failed to give full
expression to them.

"I will do anything and everything you wish,
if you will only tell me what I am to do. I'm
not afraid of anybody or anything."

"For this business you need more of discretion than courage. Through you I desire to
approach Fox Bushwell. You know him as well
as I do. I want you to sound him, so as to
ascertain whether he will deny the truth in
regard to the destruction of the bonds. In one

word, Prince, I mean to do now what I ought to have done on the day I left the city, when, maddened with the fear of dishonor, I fled like a thief. I don't blame my friends for thinking I was a thief. I acted like one ; but I wept over my own conduct before the sun went down that day."

"I am to sound him," mused Prince.

" Do it in your own way ; only be alone when you talk with him," added Mr. Longimore.

"Shall I tell you how I would sound him ?"

"Yes, tell me."

" I would hurl the truth into his teeth, fairly and squarely, without giving him a single second to invent an explanation. He lied to Mr. Doane, and he lied to all the directors."

" He certainly did ; but he is your uncle, Prince, and —"

" He is none the better for that. He has starved me and cheated me out of nearly all the comforts of life. I wish him no harm ; but he shall tell the truth. He shall go before the directors of the bank, and inform them in what manner the bonds were destroyed," added the young man, vehemently,

"You are young and full of enthusiasm, Prince. I am afraid he will not do what you expect of him. I am afraid he will deny everything, even if I should confront him again."

"He cannot."

"Perhaps he will not. If he does not, you may tell the directors where I am; or, better, come and let me know, and I will go to them."

"Suppose my uncle refuses to speak the truth, what then?" asked Prince.

"Nothing, then," said Mr. Longimore, with a shudder.

"What do you mean, sir?"

"There will then be no hope for me. Can I stand before the directors and tell them that the bonds were destroyed, when Fox Bushwell denies it? The government would not then replace them; and, under such circumstances, the bank officers would be more inclined to believe your uncle than to believe me."

"What will you do then?"

"Die then, as I would have done before, if Simon Potter had not saved me!" exclaimed Mr. Longimore, bursting into tears, and sobbing like a child.

"Not so bad as that," added the pitying Prince.

"Say no more, my friend, about that. Are my family suffering?"

"O, no; they have everything in plenty. The Dorcas Society gave your wife two hundred dollars, which they had collected to buy a boat; or, rather, lent it to them, without the knowledge of any one but the association. They shall want for nothing."

"Give my wife this letter, which I have written to-day. It is not signed; but she will know the writing. Don't lose it."

"I will not."

"Now, you will talk with your uncle to-morrow, or as soon as you can. You must wait your time, and do not be rash."

"I shall do the business as I told you, and when it is done you shall hear from me. I will come to you at night; but I may not be able to settle the matter for several days."

"I can wait a week, now that my wife and Mollie know that I am alive, and not a felon," said the cashier, sadly. "I suppose your uncle will take the furniture; or did my brother pay the note?"

"He did not. He has failed in business, and can do nothing. But my uncle shall not take the furniture, if I can help it."

"Bless you, my brave boy!" added the fugitive, pressing the warm hand he still held. "Go, now; but let me see you again as soon as you have good news for me. If you have it not, do not come. I shall understand your absence."

Prince left the house, and was immediately joined by Simon Potter, who conducted him to his boat, and bade him adieu as he pulled away towards the city. When he landed at the boat-shop, he heard the clock strike one. Half an hour later he rang the door-bell at the home of the cashier, and was admitted without delay to the dining-room, for both mother and daughter were too anxious to allow them to sleep, and had not yet retired.

CHAPTER XV.

THE HOLE IN THE CHIMNEY.

PRINCE soon told the story of his interview with the cashier, and fully explained in what manner the bonds had been destroyed.

" Wasn't it very strange that your uncle should make such a mistake?" asked Mrs. Longimore, when the young man had related the substance of the interview with her husband.

" Mr. Longimore did not think it was very strange," replied Prince. " He had done up both packages himself, in the same paper and with the same tape, so that they looked exactly alike."

" But how singular it was that, after your uncle had taken the wrong package, his house should be burned on that particular night."

Prince had not had his attention directed in this way before; and he was forced to confess that it was rather singular.

"Couldn't Mr. Bushwell see that he had the wrong bundle before he put it into the brass kettle ?" persisted Mrs. Longimore.

"It was down cellar, and in the evening. I suppose it did not occur to him that there was any possibility of its being the wrong one," replied Prince. "But I don't blame him for any mistake he made. I want to give him fair play; for, whatever mistake he made, Mr. Longimore must have made the same one when he put the wrong package into his tin box, and returned it to the vault."

"But I can't help thinking how *very* strange it was that your uncle's house was burned on that particular night, and after the mistake."

"I admit all you say ; but if the mistake had been discovered before the fire, it would not have been thought so very odd," answered Prince, who was an earnest advocate of fairness, and was unwilling that his uncle should be convicted of anything of which he was not guilty.

"Mr. Bushwell, I think, regarded the blunder and the event which followed as rather out of the common course, or he would not have told such an abominable lie about his last meeting

19

with my husband. Not a word about the burned bonds."

" Uncle Fox is a timid man; and I have no doubt he was afraid to tell the truth. But if he will tell the truth now, all may yet be well."

" This business must be very unpleasant to you, Prince. You have been very kind to us, and I am sorry it falls into your hands," added Mrs. Longimore.

" Of course I don't want to quarrel with my uncle; but I am willing to do even that for the sake of justice. I feel that Mr. Longimore is entirely innocent; and it would be a crime for me to do nothing. But now you must wait, for I may not have a chance to speak to my uncle for several days. Mrs. Pining is almost always in the house, since her best gown was burned; and I can't let her know anything about the matter."

" We can wait, now that we know father has done nothing wrong," said Mollie. " I'm sure, I feel happy again."

" So do I." added her mother. " Of course you must take your own time, Prince."

" If what you and I know were discovered,

your husband would be arrested and thrown
into prison, Mrs. Longimore. I am afraid that
uncle Fox would never tell the truth under such
circumstances. But you may be sure I will not
delay the business a day or an hour longer than
is necessary."

Prince delivered the letter, and bade them good
night, not thinking that the morning hours had
come, and walked towards home. He could not
help thinking of what the cashier's wife had
said. Though she did not say so, in so many
words, she evidently suspected that Fox Bushwell might be guilty of a greater wrong than
telling one or a dozen falsehoods. As she suggested, it was certainly very strange that the
house had been destroyed by fire on that very
night the mistake in the bank had been made.
But then, as the packages were exactly alike in
appearance, the blunder was not so very unac-
countable. The two bundles lay on the table in
the directors' room, and Fox Bushwell might
easily have picked up the wrong one. Whatever opinion Prince had of his uncle, it was not
pleasant to believe that he could be guilty of
any premeditated crime. The young man tried

to convince himself that his guardian was not a thief; but the strangeness of the circumstances troubled him.

These reflections were disturbed by his arrival at the gate of his uncle's house. He entered the yard with the utmost caution, and crept to the rear of the lot. Placing a flour barrel, which had been left behind the house, under it, he prepared to get in at the window by which he had made his egress nearly five hours before. He recognized the danger of an accident, which might alarm his uncle, and perhaps arouse the whole neighborhood. He had no talent for lying and deception, and he was not even willing to invent a story to satisfy his uncle, in the emergency of being discovered. He was sure he could silence him by alluding to the bonds; but he was not willing to do this under such unfavorable circumstances. These considerations only made him the more careful when he mounted the flour-barrel and raised the window. At this point he took the precaution to remove his shoes.

Fortunately, Fox Bushwell and the housekeeper slept soundly; or, if they did not, Prince made so little noise that it would have been impossible for them to hear him. Closing the window behind him, he crept into the kitchen. The difficult part of the enterprise was to ascend the stairs, for the weight of a person caused them to creak. To prevent this, Prince kept close to the wall, where the string-piece was nailed to the studs, thus avoiding the strain on the weaker side. By taking a long time for the ascent, he effected it in safety, and stealthily as a mouse crawled into his chamber, the door of which he had left open. He listened, and could hear the snoring of the weary money-lender. In a few moments he was in bed, but not yet to sleep. The events of the night had been too exciting to permit him to slumber for a time.

He thought over what had occurred in the Northport woods; and then his mind went back to the night of the fire, when the bonds had been destroyed. He recalled all the events of that evening. Naturally enough the startling features of the affair came first to his mind — the cry of fire which had roused him from his deep sleep. He had waked his uncle, helped dress him, and then hurried him out of the

house. Certainly, the old man was fast asleep
when he called him; he had no doubt of that.
A man so timid as he could not lie in his bed
while the smoke and the flames were creeping up
to him. But all the events subsequent to the
breaking out of the conflagration were patent to
everybody in the neighborhood. The trembling
and groaning of the miser in the street had been
seen and heard by the neighbors in the light of
the fire. But what had happened before the
smoke had wakened him? This was a more
important inquiry on the part of Prince.

"Let me see," said he to himself. "I went
to bed about ten. I was down stairs just before,
and uncle Fox was in the cellar. There was
nothing very odd about that, for he cuts up the
kindlings for the fire every evening before he
goes to bed. I went to bed; but the tea, which
had become stronger, or the Latin that bothered
me, kept me awake. Why didn't I think of
this before? I heard the clock strike twelve
before uncle Fox went to his room, and then
he came up as still as a mouse. I thought he
was more considerate than usual, for I am sure
he came up stairs in his stocking feet. I dropped

asleep then; but the fire must have broken out in less than half an hour, for the whole concern was burned down when the clock struck one. Uncle Fox has told everybody he went to bed about half past ten that night; but I know he didn't go till after twelve. Why should he lie about it?"

Prince could not imagine why the old man, who was a clergyman, too, should lie. There seemed to be no occasion for a falsehood. Then the wakeful young man recalled other incidents since the fire, especially the hearing of the hammer, on the night the family moved, in the cellar. Prince had gone down stairs to ascertain the cause of the noise, and found that his uncle was at work in the cellar. He was filling up a hole in the chimney near its foundation at the bottom of the cellar, which affected the draught, causing the flue to smoke. That was the explanation the old man gave of the nature of his night job. Prince could not see how a hole in the chimney four or five feet below the stove flue, could affect the draught; but Fox Bushwell had been a brick-mason once, and he ought to know.

Of course, if his uncle said so, the draught must have been affected; and it was quite decent and proper to fill up the hole which made the mischief, especially as the old man had bricks and mortar, and knew how to do it. Prince was a boy, and had a boy's curiosity; and, as any boy would have done, he went down cellar to see how and where the job had been done. He had found the arch, on one side of which the aperture had been closed, filled with old rubbish, just as though Fox Bushwell did not care to have his handiwork inspected, though he had learned the mason's trade. It seemed just as though the work had been covered up, so that no one should see where the hole had been stopped. Besides, Prince was of the opinion, whether right or wrong, that a hole below the stove-flue in the kitchen would not affect the draught. The cook-stove had worked very well the first day it was set up, so far as he could remember.

"Uncle Fox, it seems from Mr. Longimore's story, had a place in the cellar of the old house where he kept his valuable papers," Prince reasoned to himself. "He kept them in an old

brass kettle; and when he brought the package
from the bank, he put it into this kettle, and
stowed it away in the wall. He laid up his
treasure in the cellar. He put the bonds into
it, and they were burned. If he stopped to
look at the package, he must have seen the
label on it. Perhaps he looked at it, and perhaps he didn't. If he had a place in the old
cellar to keep his papers, why shouldn't he have
one in the new cellar? The question before the
house just now is, whether or not that place in
the foundation of the chimney isn't the safe for
uncle Fox's papers. If he lied to the directors
about the meeting with the cashier that morning; if he lied to everybody about the time he
went to bed on the night of the fire, there must
be something worth lying for. I should rather
like to know what's in the hole in the chimney,
if anything. I will know, too. There are bricks
and mortar in the cellar, and if I can get those
two bricks out, I can put them in well enough,
especially if they are to be covered up with
rubbish.

"When can I do it? It won't be safe for
me to dig out the bricks when uncle Fox is in

the house, for he will hear me.   He is out of
the house a good part of the day; but then Mrs.
Pining is in it.   The more I think of it, the
better satisfied I am that I ought to know
what's in that hole before I say anything to my
precious guardian about the bonds.   If he happened by any possible chance to save them from
the fire, and stowed them away in the hole in
in the chimney, he will remove them if I say
anything."

Thus thinking and thus talking to himself,
he went to sleep from sheer exhaustion, and
without any attempt to do so.   He that talks to
himself generally talks to a fool; but this is not
always true.   Prince's talk to himself rather
cheered him; and he felt that he was talking to
a pretty smart fellow on this occasion.   He believed that he had got an idea.   Fox Bushwell
would lie any time for twenty-five cents, and of
course for forty thousand dollars he would tell
as many lies as twenty-five cents goes into forty
thousand, if his life lasted long enough for him
to do so.

Prince slept and slept after- the excitement
and fatigue of the night.   He did not hear his

uncle call him, and he did not hear Mrs. Pining call him. He did not awake till the clock struck nine, when his nap seemed to end by limitation. He dressed himself rather mechanically, going over all the reflections which had occupied his mind before he went to sleep. As people often find it, his views were not half so firm and fixed in the daylight as they had been in the darkness, and much of the reasoning which was strong before, was weak now. Still he was determined at the first opportunity to explore that hole in the arch of the chimney. He had a suspicion, and it seemed to be a duty either to convict or acquit his uncle of the supposed wrong.

"Sufferin,' dyin' world!" groaned Mrs. Pining, when he appeared in the kitchen, where his breakfast was waiting for him. "I thought you was goin' to lay abed all day!"

"I was tired, and couldn't go to sleep when I went to bed," pleaded Prince. "Where is uncle Fox?"

"Gone to see the insurance folks," snapped the housekeeper. "I want my money to buy some things, and I can't git none on't till the

insurance is paid. I hain't got nothin' to wear.
I can't go out o' the house; and Sabba' day
comin', and I can't go to meetin', nor nothin'.
Folks lay abed all day, so I can't get time to
do nothin', nuther."

"I don't generally lie abed so late."

"Well, you needn't complain about your
victuals; it's been standin' two hours waitin' for
you. If I wanted to go out and buy some things,
I can't git no time to go."

"I will not find any fault when I lie abed as
late as I did this morning," replied Prince,
seating himself at the table.

The young man ate his breakfast, and left the
house. During the day he attended to his duties
as instructor of the boat clubs. The next day
he was up betimes in the morning, so that the
housekeeper had no reason to complain of him.
When he went into the kitchen, Mrs. Pining
was reproaching her employer for not paying
her interest, and setting forth her need of "sunthin' to wear;" but the insurance folks had not
paid him, and he was not ready to meet the
demand.

"You can give me sunthin'—can't you?"

whined the widow. "Can't you let me have fifteen dollars?"

"That's more money than I have in the house, Mrs. Pining," replied Fox Bushwell. "I expect to get my insurance by to-morrow, and then I will pay you the forty-eight dollars. I can't do it before. You mustn't be hard upon me, after all I've lost."

"Dyin' world! What's goin' to become on me, if I don't go to meetin'? I feel jest like a heathen, now."

"Wait a few days, and I'll try to raise the money for you."

"Lud's sake! That's jest what you've been sayin' ever sence the fire. Sufferin' and dyin' in sin and iniquity! without nothin' to wear, and no chance to go to meetin'!"

"Prince, have you seen Longimore's folks lately?" asked Fox Bushwell, as his ward entered the kitchen.

"I have seen them every day."

"How do they seem?"

"Better than they were."

"I'm glad to hear it. I don't like to do anything hard; but I don't see how I can help it," whined the money lender.

"What are you going to do, uncle Fox?" asked Prince, his heart rising into his throat, as much with indignation as with fear.

"To-morrow it will be ten days since Longimore went off; and all that furniture will belong to me then."

"But you will not take it away from them — will you?"

"What on earth can I do? I can't afford to lose six hundred and twenty dollars. It would ruin me."

"But you can afford to wait a few. days," pleaded Prince.

"What's the use of waiting? Longimore's brother can't do anything for his folks. The furniture will belong to me to-morrow; and I think I know where I can sell it for enough to make me whole. Currier is going to house-keeping soon, and wanted to buy Captain Seaboard's; but when he saw it, he said it wasn't good enough for him. I shall see him to-day; and if you go to Longimore's house, I wish you would just ask his wife if she has any objection to my showing him the things this afternoon. If she has, I shall take him in to-morrow."

"I think you had better keep quiet for a few days, uncle Fox," said Prince, choking down his indignation.

"Keep quiet?"

"At least till you get your insurance. People are sorry for Mrs. Longimore and her children, whatever they think of her husband; and if you should take her furniture away from her, it would excite the indignation of people against you."

"But I can't afford to lose my customer," said Fox Bushwell, evidently alarmed.

"If you do anything of this kind, the insurance people won't pay you as long as they can help doing so."

"Currier has offered me seven hundred cash for that furniture, without seeing it. That includes the piano, of course. But I expect to get eight hundred."

"And you mean to make nearly two hundred dollars out of Mr. Longimore's misfortunes?" added Prince, his eyes flashing.

"Of course I'm going to get as much as I can for it."

"You won't sell it, uncle Fox," replied Prince, unable to contain himself any longer.

"Do you think not, Prince?"

"I know you won't. If no one else inter-feres, I will. I can stop it, I know."

"Do you want to ruin me, Prince?"

"No sir; and I don't want you to ruin any one else. Your bill of sale is good for nothing."

"Good for nothing!" gasped the miser.

"No; at least, I believe it is not, and a certain lawyer says there is doubt enough about it to hang a lawsuit on."

"Good Heaven! What do you mean?" groaned Fox Bushwell.

"Most people believe Mr. Longimore is dead, and that he has been dead nine days. Your bill of sale is dated to-morrow, and of course he could not sign it ten days after he was dead."

"Am I to lose my money?" whined the miser.

"I don't know; but the lawyers won't let you take the furniture to-morrow. Mrs. Longimore has taken legal advice, and feels safe for a while," replied Prince, satisfied that he had carried his point.

Fox Bushwell groaned in bitterness of spirit. He did not like lawyers. They were an expen-

sive luxury. He did not attempt to take the
furniture on the tenth day, but after breakfast
he did go to a legal gentleman with the note
and bill of sale. As soon as he had gone, Mrs.
Pining opened, as usual, in regard to her unpaid
interest, which she certainly needed.

" I will lend you fifteen dollars," said Prince,
who had about this amount left of his two
months' allowance.

" Sufferin', dyin'! You, Prince?"

He produced the money, and she promised
to repay it as soon as her interest was received.
She bustled about in great haste, and went to
one of the neighbors to borrow garments enough
in which to do her shopping.

" Lock the house, and put the key of the
back door under the step, if you go out, Prince,"
said she, as she left the house.

Prince did lock the door, but he did not put
the key under the step. He locked all the doors
and fastened all the windows. Then he went
down cellar, and removed the rubbish from the
arch. The day before he had seen his uncle
take a note from the package which was so like
the bundle of bonds, and which had been put

20

in the old secretary saved from the fire. That bundle of papers was not concealed in the cellar, at any rate.

The mortar of the two bricks which Fox Bushwell had laid in the arch was not very hard, because the cellar was quite damp. With the trowel he succeeded in digging it all out of the interstices. With much labor, and no little skill, he removed the first brick, and then the second. Afraid that his uncle might return, he thrust his arm into the aperture, and felt about for any article the cavity might contain. His hand touched something smooth and soft He drew it forth. It was a package enveloped in thin rubber cloth. With eager, trembling hands he unfolded it, removing several newspaper wrappers after the covering of rubber cloth. At last he reached a package which was the counterpart of the bundle of valuable papers he had seen in the hands of his uncle. The label indicated that it contained bonds; and a further examination convinced him that this was the package which Fox Bushwell had brought from the bank — by mistake.

" The precious old villain!" muttered Prince,

as he rolled up the bundle again, just as he had found it; but he did not restore it to the hole in the chimney.

Softening the mortar in the tub, he relaid the two bricks, and rubbed down the wall till it looked as it had before. Restoring the rubbish as his uncle had placed it, he left the cellar with the bonds in his pocket What should he do with them?

CHAPTER XVI.

THE PRESIDENT'S LETTER.

TO say that Prince Willingood was almost beside himself with joy, on the one hand, when he thought of the triumphant vindication of Mollie's father, and with pity and detestation, on the other, when he thought of his uncle, is expressing his feelings only very mildly. He had not believed that Fox Bushwell was either wicked or brave enough to commit a great crime. The story of the brass kettle and the burning of whatever it contained, were mere inventions; and now that the bonds were safe, he could not help asking the hard question, how it was that anything happened to be burned. If by one remarkable chance the bonds were in the cellar, and by another equally remarkable chance the house was burned while they were there, it was not likely that, when it appeared that the bonds were not there, the burning of the house was the simple result of a blind fate.

Prince had his doubts, and they troubled him sorely; for, whatever else Fox Bushwell might be, he was the young man's uncle. Why had the old man taken so much pains on that particular evening to show the cashier that he kept his valuable papers in a brass kettle, concealed in the cellar wall? He could not resist the conclusion, much as he desired to do so, that the house had been burned in order to cover the loss of the bonds. Of course he could not have anticipated the disappearance of the cashier on the morning after the fire; but the evidence would have been just as convincing to the directors as to Mr. Longimore. He took the bonds by mistake, as the presence of his own private papers at the bank would show; he had put them where he usually kept his own most valuable documents; and now they were destroyed. Turn it over in whatever way he might, Prince could not help believing that his uncle had intended to do a great wrong.

Boy as he was, he had right views in regard to his duty. He had positively refused to take part in the concealment of Mr. Longimore's possible crime, and could he do less in regard to that of Fox Bushwell? Badly as his uncle had treated him, until driven by the fear of consequences to do better, the nephew was actuated by no spirit of revenge. He would gladly save his uncle from exposure and punishment; but it must rest with the directors of the bank to proceed as they thought best. Some of them were also stockholders and directors in the insurance company which refused to settle the money-lender's claim for his loss.

In the privacy of his chamber Prince removed the wrappers from the bundle he had taken from the hole in the chimney, and satisfied himself that it contained the bonds. He even counted the amount of them and found it corresponded with that of the lost package. And then again came the question, what should he do with them. He could not keep them in the house, and he dared not carry them down to the retreat of the exiled cashier, lest they should be lost by the upsetting of the boat, or some other accident, which, under other circumstances, he would not have regarded as even possible. The salvation of the cashier depended upon the restoration of the package to the bank; and he could not risk a single chance of failure to do his whole duty. But, whatever was done, Mrs. Longimore and Mollie ought to have the good news at once — the good news which would restore to them the husband and father without the stain of crime.

Prince wrapped up the bonds again just as he had found them in the hole in the chimney, and went out of the house at the back door. This time, when he had locked it, he put the key under the step. The package of bonds was in the breast pocket of his coat, and he kept one hand upon it every moment of the time he was in the street on his way to the cashier's home. He was promptly admitted, as he always was. Mrs. Longimore and Mollie were more cheerful than they had been before for a fortnight, for the cashier was not dead, and there was a chance that his innocence might be proved.

Prince's eyes glowed when he entered the house, for he was intensely excited; as who would not have been under such circumstances? Mrs. Longimore at once concluded that he had fought the great battle with his uncle.

"You have done it, Prince, I see by your looks," said Mrs. Longimore.

"Done what?" asked he.

"Talked with your uncle. You have told him what you said you should."

"No, I have not. I have not said a word to him, and I don't intend to do so now."

"You said you should tell him squarely that he knew all about the bonds," added the lady, perplexed and disappointed by his change of front. "I am sure my husband has told you the truth."

"I know he has," replied Prince, warmly.

"And he depends upon you to help him prove his innocence."

"Not in vain has he depended upon me. I have done better than I could by talking with my uncle," answered the young man, proudly.

"Why, what do you mean?"

"I have found the bonds."

"Found them!" gasped Mrs. Longimore.

"You don't mean so, Prince!" exclaimed Mollie.

"But I do," he added, taking them from his pocket, and tossing the bundle on the table.

WITH EAGER, TREMBLING HANDS HE UNFOLDED IT.   Page 306.

"There they are — every bond, just as they came from the bank. Mr. Longimore can come back now as soon as he pleases."

"Why, Prince!" cried Mollie, clasping her hands with delight.

"My dear boy, you have saved us all," added the mother.

"I have done the best I could."

"Angels could no more," said Mollie.

"Did your uncle give you the package? Has he repented? Has he changed his mind?" asked Mrs. Longimore.

"He did not give them to me, and he has had no chance to repent or to change his mind. He knows nothing at all of what I have done, and doubtless believes the package is just where he left it," replied Prince. "It all looks like a plain case to you; but I am sorely bothered. I don't know what to do."

"It seems to me you have done everything already," suggested Mrs. Longimore.

"But there are two sides to this question. Your husband is one side, and my uncle is the other. The burden has been shifted from Mr. Longimore to Fox Bushwell," Prince explained.

"If I don't hand these bonds over to the bank, the directors will arrest your husband when he comes back; if I do hand them over, they will arrest my uncle. I brought them here, because I want you to advise me what to do."

"I suppose there is only one way, and that is, to do right," replied the cashier's wife.

"We don't always know what is right."

"You have not told me where you got the bonds, Prince."

"I will tell you all about it. On the night after the fire I heard a clicking noise down stairs. I went into the kitchen, and found my uncle was at work on the chimney in the cellar. I thought nothing of it then; but after I had seen Mr. Longimore, I had some suspicions. This morning, when uncle Fox and Mrs. Pining were absent, I took out two bricks in the chimney, and found the bonds. That's the whole story. I put this and that together, and found that two and two made four. That's the reason I thought of seeing what ailed that chimney."

"I wanted to ask you to search the house, Prince, for I did not think the mistake in the package, and the burning of the house, were two things that were likely to happen in the same night; but I did not like to ask you to do so," added Mrs. Longimore.

"That was just my own thought. I am afraid the fire was not an accident. I heard uncle Fox tell, a year ago or more how a man set his barn on fire, and was ten miles away when the flames burst out. He fixed a candle in the hay, in such a way that it would burn two hours before the fire got down to the hay. I shouldn't wonder if he set his own house on fire in the same way, for he was fast asleep when I called him."

"Perhaps he was."

"I had hard work to wake him."

"That was part of the play, it may be."

"I can easily believe it was. The insurance company have not paid the loss yet, and keep putting him off," added Prince. "I think the officers suspect that something is wrong. But what are we to do with these bonds? That's the question now."

"I can advise only one thing, Prince," said Mrs. Longimore. "I should not be willing to have them over night in this house."

"I should not in my uncle's; and I don't like to carry them down to Mr. Longimore, for fear some accident might happen," added Prince.

"Why not carry them to the bank?" asked Mollie, who could not see the necessity of doing anything short of what was exactly right.

"I don't want to make it any worse for my uncle than is necessary. If I had done what I felt, at first, that I ought to do, I should have informed Mr. Doane of what Simon Potter had told me. Then they would have arrested Mr. Longimore, and the bonds might never have been found. Of course the whole truth must come out; but I wish to spare uncle Fox as much as possible without doing anything wrong. I will tell you what I will do: I will ask Mr. Doane to come over here; we will tell him the whole story, and then do just as he says."

This proposition met with favor; and Mrs. Longimore wrote a note to the president of the bank, which Mollie carried to him. Mr. Doane returned with her.

"I suppose all the people at the bank believe that my husband took those bonds, Mr. Doane," said Mrs. Longimore, when the president was seated.

"We tried hard to believe that he did not. You know we always held him in the highest respect and regard, and we are only sorry now that we had not raised his salary, and thus removed, in part at least, any temptation for him to do anything wrong," replied the president. "We never heard till since he left he was in debt or in trouble. If he had only asked for more salary, we should certainly have granted it. As it is, we feel a little to blame for not doing so."

"You are certainly very kind to make any allowance for him; but I wish to say that my husband would not steal under any temptation," added the wife.

"I hope not."

"I am sure of it," continued Mrs. Longimore, taking the bundle of bonds from the table. "Will you be kind enough to open that package?"

Mr. Doane removed the several coverings, and opened his eyes very wide when he came to the familiar wrapper, red tape, and label of the lost bonds. Though he did not say so, the sight of the package convinced him that the cashier could steal, and had stolen, them, either with or without the temptation of a burden of private debts. Finding them in the house of the absent official seemed to be evidence that he had stolen them.

"I am very glad indeed to recover these bonds," said he, "not only for the sake of the bank, but for Mr. Longimore's sake. I assure you the people of the bank have no ill will towards your husband, madam; and since the property has been restored, I think I can guarantee that they will not prosecute him."

"Mr. Longimore knows no more about those bonds than you did ten minutes ago, Mr. Doane," interposed Prince, warmly, for he did not like the cool tone of the proceedings. "He did not steal them, did not take them, did not hide them, did not do anything with them. He is as innocent as you are, sir."

"I'm sure I hope he is," protested the president.

"I know he is!" exclaimed the young man.

"I am glad you are so well informed, my young friend," added Mr. Doane, with a smile at the earnestness of the speaker. "If Mr. Longimore had not — had not left, doubtless the affair would have presented a different aspect. Perhaps you had better. let Mrs. Longimore explain the circumstances under which the bonds came into her possession."

The president was a little dry, and rather sarcastic, in his manner towards Prince, who appeared to be meddling with what did not concern him.

" Prince brought them here just before I sent for you," said Mrs. Longimore, promptly.

" Ah! indeed!" added Mr. Doane, feeling now that the young man had a right to speak.

Prince did speak. He said that Mr. Longimore was alive, that he had told him just what had passed between himself and Fox Bushwell, and related in detail his own suspicions, and the manner in which he had taken the bonds from the hole in the chimney, within the hour in which he spoke. Of course Mr. Doane was interested. The story was plausible, and the bundle of bonds in his hands fully confirmed it.

" I am sorry for your uncle," said the president.

"So am I, sir; but I have told the whole truth, without regard to him or any one else," replied Prince.

"You are entitled to a great deal of credit for what you have done, and the directors will not forget that these bonds have been recovered through your agency. How guilty Mr. Bushwell was I cannot say. If he really made a mistake, and took the wrong package from the bank by accident, and then was tempted to keep them, when the error was discovered, it is a little better than if he purposely took the bonds from the bank, as, I confess I am afraid he did. Either was bad enough."

"I didn't think uncle Fox was villian enough to do such a thing," added Prince. "I had some trouble with him a while ago; but that grew out of his meanness only. Now I wish you would tell me what to do, Mr. Doane."

"I think you need do nothing, Prince. You have done enough. But this matter opens another. I am one of the directors of the insurance company which took the risk on your uncle's house. We generally settle losses at once. But we had some doubts in Mr. Bush-

well's case. We have not been able to get hold
of the facts, for his statements do not exactly
coincide with each other. I need not say that
your account of the bonds makes the matter ten
times worse for him."

"In a word, you believe that my uncle set
fire to his own house to get the insurance," added
Prince.

" We have not said that we believed he did
so. That would place it a little too strong. If
the fire caught from his lamp, and he went to
bed at half past ten, it would have broken out
before midnight. We do not believe it was set
on fire, for no one could have thrown a match
into the heap of shavings, where the fire started,
on that side of the house, for there was no cellar window there."

" My uncle did not go to bed that night till after
twelve," added Prince, explaining the events connected with the fire.

" Then your uncle has not told us the truth,
though the truth would have served his purpose
better than a falsehood. If he had said the fire
had broken out fifteen or twenty minutes after
he left the cellar, we could have understood that

21

he was careless with his lamp. He insured the house only a short time before it was burned, though he never paid a dollar for insurance before. There are other circumstances which make the case doubtful."

"Since Prince told my husband's story, I have felt sure that Mr. Bushwell set his house on fire to make it appear that the bonds were burned," added Mrs. Longimore. "At any rate, Mr. Longimore believed they were burned, and this belief made him almost crazy."

"It was a terribly trying situation for him, especially after he had pledged all his furniture to enable him to pay the sum he had overdrawn, which he need not have done. He charged every dollar he took; and if we had known the circumstances, we should have raised his salary, instead of censuring him.

"But I want to tell him that the bonds are safe," said Prince. "The poor man is in misery now, and this news will rejoice him. What shall I say to him from you?" asked the young man, anxiously.

"The directors will be in session this forenoon. Come to the bank in half an hour,

Prince, and I will tell you what to say to him.
I hope and believe it will be a message you will
delight to carry to him."

"And what is to be done with my uncle?"

"I don't know yet. The insurance people
meet to-morrow, to settle your uncle's and other
losses. We intend to question Mr. Bushwell
again; and after what you have said I can do
so more intelligently than before. On the whole,
I think we had better not mention anything that
has occurred. We will keep it all from the public,
at least till to-morrow. You will not say anything to your uncle, Prince — not a word; but
some one will keep an eye on him hereafter."

Mr. Doane left the house, and hastened to
the bank, where he arrived just in season to
preside at the meeting of the directors, at ten
o'clock. He was hardly gone before Minnie
Darling and Nellie Patterdale called.

"Is Prince Willingood here?" asked Minnie,
when Mollie went to the door.

"He is," she replied.

"He is a pretty professor of the art of rowing," pouted Minnie. "It is after ten o'clock;
the two new boats — the Lily and the Psyche

—are already in the water, and we want our instructor."

"He has been very busy for us this morning. He is exceedingly kind to us; and if he is late, I hope you will excuse him," pleaded Mollie; and there was a smile on her face, as sweet as it was unwonted of late.

" Then he is certainly excused," added Nellie.

" But won't you go with us, Mollie ? " asked Minnie. " You are the leader of our boat, you know."

" Perhaps I will go; but I don't know anything about rowing, you are aware."

" Prince will show you all about it; and I'm sure he never did a pleasanter duty in his life," added Minnie, encouraged by the smile of her friend. "I hope you will go."

" Come in, and I will ask mother."

" Ah, Professor Willingood, have you forgotten the duties of your office ? " asked Minnie, as they entered the room where Prince was.

"I confess that I did forget them; but I was very busy about important business," pleaded he.

"You are forgiven, at Mollie's request."

"I'm afraid I can't be with you this forenoon, for I have to go to Northport."

"Indeed you must be with us, professor. We have four boats afloat, and we need you. Can't you take all the boats to Northport with you?"

"Perhaps I can."

"And Mollie will go, too."

"Can I, mother?" asked she.

"Certainly you can. You need the air, for you have hardly been out of the house for a fortnight."

"Then I shall go, by all means," laughed Prince.

"I knew you would."

"You can bring a passenger back with you," added the instructor of rowing, with a significant glance at Mrs. Longimore and her daughter.

"Who? Not that wild man with the conic section on his head?"

"No; but if the passenger is ready to come, you shall see who it is," replied Prince. "Now, if you will, go down to the shop, and take your places in the boats, I will be there in a few moments; or you can pull about till I get there."

The girls hastened away to the shore, rejoiced to have Mollie with them for the first time. Prince went to the bank ten minutes earlier than the time he had been requested to be there; but the action in regard to the cashier had been taken, and Mr. Doane was writing a letter to him, which he handed to the messenger.

"Give this to Mr. Longimore, Prince," said the president. "We have raised his salary five hundred dollars a year, so as to cover the last two years. We have invited him to return to his place at once."

"That's handsome, sir," exclaimed Prince, as much rejoiced as though the hundred dollars of back pay was to go into his own pocket.

"More than this, Prince; the bank has recognized your important services in recovering the bonds by a grant of five thousand dollars."

"I object sir!" protested Prince. "You must give the money to Mr. Longimore. I don't want it; I am rich; I have an income of eighteen hundred a year. If you will only give it to the cashier to pay his debts, I shall be ten times as much obliged to you."

"Do you hear what this young fellow says?" laughed the president, turning to the directors.

They did not hear; but Mr. Doane explained. Prince argued, when they protested; and by sheer begging at last he induced them to comply.

"Mr. Longimore can draw his back pay as soon as he returns," added Mr. Doane.

"Suppose you put it all together in one check, and enclose it in this letter?" suggested Prince.

The president complied; and the letter, after the addition of a postscript and the check, was given to him. The messenger hastened with a light heart to join the boat-clubs.

CHAPTER XVII.

THE CLUBS PULL TO NORTHPORT.

WHEN Prince reached the pier in front of
the boat-shop, four of the five clubs
were seated in the boat, pulling about near the
shore. Mollie had her place in the Dorcas, and
had already made considerable progress in learning her duty as leader, under the direction of
Minnie, who was at the stroke oar. The two
new boats could not be distinguished from the
old ones, except by reading the name on the
stern or bows. The weather was mild and pleasant, and there was hardly a ripple on the bay
between the city and Turk Head.

"Dorcas ahoy!" shouted Prince.

"Won't you go with us, Professor Willingood?" asked Kitty Jones, mischievously, as the
Lily Club pulled by the pier.

"No, I thank you; I must go in the Dorcas,"
replied the instructor.

"Of course you must!" laughed Kitty. "Where Mollie Longimore is, the professor must be."

"She hasn't learned to row yet," pleaded Prince.

"She is the leader of the Dorcas Club, and she need not learn," added Jennie Waite. "That's only an excuse."

"Well, it's a good excuse," replied Prince, as the Dorcas approached, and he took his place by the side of Mollie Longimore, in the stern-sheets.

All the boats gathered together near the pier, to obtain their instructions. Before Prince could give them, each of the leaders in her boat produced a flag, and began to wave it vigorously above her head. This demonstration appeared to be intended to surprise the instructor, and of course he gallantly expressed his astonishment at this sudden display of the colors. Some of the girls thought that a boat without a flag was like a man without a country, and they had supplied the deficiency without mentioning the matter to Prince. The flags were very pretty, certainly. The ground of each was white silk, crossed diagonally, like the Russian man-of-war ensign, with another color, which in the Dorcas's was red, in the Lily's yellow, in the Undine's blue, and in the Psyche's green. Don John had placed a couple of small eye-bolts in the stern of each boat for the flag-staff.

"Professor Willingood, we greet you," said Carrie West, in the Psyche.

"Thank you. If this demonstration was in-tended as a salute to me, I acknowledge the compliment," replied Prince, removing his hat, bowing as gracefully as the occasion seemed to require.

"Of course we could not hoist the flag till the commodore came on board," added Minnie.

"I shall not arrogate to myself so high-sound-ing a title as that; but I suggest that you will need such a personage to regulate the move-ments of the fleet," continued Prince. "It gives me very great pleasure to be able to say that you row exceedingly well, and that you handle your boats very skilfully. There is a great vari-ety of movements which may be made by the fleet. With four boats, you may row in a sin-gle line, two abreast, or four abreast. This fore-noon we will confine our attention to these changes. If we had five boats we could do better."

"I hope we shall have another boat soon," said Kitty Jones, nervously, for she was full of excitement.

"As we have but four, we will make the best of them," replied Prince. "Let us understand how to make the changes before we start. We will go off in a single line, in this order: Dorcas, Lily, Undine, Psyche. At the word, 'By twos,' the first and third boats will cease rowing, the second boat will pull alongside the first, and the fourth alongside the third. Then the third and fourth will close up, and each boat that stops rowing will commence again as soon as the other boat is abreast of her."

"But we may not hear the order in the fourth boat," suggested Carrie West.

"Then we will give the word by signal," replied Prince, picking up the boat-hook, and fastening his handkerchief to the end of it. "I will raise the signal, and hold it upright till all the leaders are sure to see it; then I will drop it twice to the left for the order of 'By twos.'"

"That will be nice!" said Kate Bilder.

"All ready, then; follow the Dorcas," added Prince.

The Dorcas led the way, and the boats were soon in a single line, headed towards the Northport shore. The girls pulled with remarkable precision, keeping the slow and measured stroke required of them. After the fleet had gone a little way, Prince elevated the signal, holding it up for a couple of minutes. It was seen, for all the leaders were on the lookout for it; but none of the rowers could see it, of course, as they sat back to it. Dropping it twice to the left, the first and third boats lay upon their oars, and the second and fourth pulled to the left, as directed, till the four were in pairs, and all gave way again. It was pretty well done, for the first attempt. It was repeated several times, till the instructor was satisfied, and then the four clubs were called together for another "powwow."

"We need some more signals," said Prince. "When I wave this flag in a circle around my head," — and he suited the action to the word, — "you will all come together, as we are now. When I drop it once to the left, it means 'sin-

gle line ;' when I drop it four times, alternately
to the left and right, it means 'by fours.' To
change from twos to fours, the Psyche will go
to the left of the Lily, and the Undine to the
right of the Dorcas, the two boats in the front
line lying on their oars till the other two come
alongside."

The instructor repeated his explanation till all
the leaders understood it, and then the boats
went off in single line. The signal "by twos"
was then given, and the movement very well
executed. While in this order, the signal was
elevated and dropped four times. The leaders
of the Dorcas and the Lily gave the order for
the rowers to lie on their oars, while those of
the Undine and the Psyche steered their boats
towards the positions assigned to them. Unfortunately, the rear boats were too near the front
rank, and could not turn short enough to clear
the head boats. Prince gave the signal to come
together, upon this failure, and instructed the
rowers of the Dorcas and Lily not to stop, but
to pull slowly, while those in the Undine and
Psyche were to pull rapidly. The experiment
was repeated, and was a success. The girls were

delighted with the result, which was improved by practice.

To pass from "fours" to "twos," and from "twos" to a single line, the orders were reversed. These manœuvres were executed several times, and the fair rowists were intensely interested in them, so much so that they gave their whole attention, which is required in order to do anything well. Mollie Longimore was an apt scholar under the tuition of Prince, and before the fleet reached the Northport shore she was able to give all the orders. As the boats approached the mouth of Little River, the instructor gave the signal for "single line," and the Dorcas led the way into the inlet.

"Way enough!" said Mollie, prompted by Prince.

The oars were tossed and boated as required. The rest of the fleet came into the little bay, but kept well off the shore.

"Now, if you will excuse Mollie, and me for half an hour, we will attend to the matter which brought us here," said Prince, as he swung the Dorcas around till her stern-sheet were abreast a flat rock. "You can row till we return; and I will hail you when we are ready to go back to the city."

"But we want Mollie to act as leader," replied Minnie.

"You should learn to pull without any one to steer," laughed Prince; "and this will be a good time for you to make a beginning. When there is no coxswain in the boat, she is under the command of the one at the stroke oar."

"We will try it," added Minnie, though she could not help wondering why Prince wanted Mollie to go on shore with him.

Prince assisted the leader to the rock, and they walked away from the shore together. The boats pulled out of the cove, and the crew of the Dorcas proceeded to experiment in rowing without the use of the rudder. Mollie was not less astonished than her friends had been at the invitation to land, though she surmised the meaning of it.

"Where are we going, Prince?" she asked.

"To see your father," he replied, "and to take him back to the city. He is the passenger of whom I spoke."

"Are you sure it is safe for him to return?" added Mollie, with emotion.

"It is quite safe. He can take his place in the bank again to-day, if he chooses."

Prince led the way to the house of Simon Potter; but that vigilant sentinel presented himself before them, to intercept their progress, when they had accomplished but half the distance.

"It is all right, Simon Potter," said Prince. "This is Mr. Longimore's daughter, and he will be glad enough to see her."

"But —"

"No butting is necessary. I want the cashier to go back with me, and take his place in the bank," interposed the enthusiastic messenger.

"This is some trick," suggested Simon Potter.

"No it isn't."

"You ain't nothin' but a boy, and 'taint very diffikilt to cheat one like you."

"In one word then, the bonds have come to light, and I have a letter from the president of the bank to Mr. Longimore. I know it's all right."

"I'm glad on't."

"Let us see the cashier as quick as you can."

"MOLLIE! MY DAUGHTER!" EXCLAIMED HE, FOLDING HER IN HIS ARMS. Page 337.

Simon Potter led the way to the little barn adjoining his house. It contained a cow-stable, and a mow, which had, perhaps a ton of hay on it. But the cashier did not appear to be within the building.

"Mr. Longimore!" said the strange man.

"Where is he?" asked Prince, his curiosity somewhat excited.

"He ain't fur off," replied Simon Potter, repeating the cashier's name twice more.

When he had pronounced it the third time, there was a movement in the hay in the mow, and Mr. Longimore crawled out from the mass, apparently from under the weight of the whole of it.

"Mollie! my daughter!" exclaimed he, folding her in his arms, while the tears coursed down his pale, sunken cheeks.

"O, father! I'm so glad to see you again!" and she wept with him.

For some time they remained weeping and sobbing in each other's embrace. The cashier trembled with emotion, for he had not expected to see his daughter so soon, and in that place.

"I don't exactly see how he could live under

all that hay," said Prince, leaving the father and daughter to themselves for a time.

"You needn't tell nobody on't," replied Simon Potter. "I made that place for myself; but I never happened to want it for nothin'. Folks don't bother me much."

The strange man took the fork and removed a portion of the loose hay on the edge of the mow, and a hole appeared. To satisfy himself, Prince crawled into it and found quite an apartment there. It had been made by laying the hay on each side of it, and then placing some rails across it, on which more hay had been piled up, till the sticks were entirely concealed. Light and air could be obtained at the rear of the den, at the pleasure of the occupant. Prince thought it was a nice place.

It was said that when people called to see Simon Potter, he could seldom be found, either within his house or on his farm. Sometimes, if the visitor called out his business aloud, the strange man would mysteriously make his appearance, though a moment before nothing could be found of him. The young man concluded that he often hid himself in this den to avoid meeting visitors. And I wish to add that this incident is not "made out of whole cloth," for such a person actually existed not far from the locality indicated.

"Why are you here, Mollie?" asked Mr. Longimore, choking with emotion, when Prince crawled out of the den.

"I brought her here, sir; and you need not give yourself another moment of uneasiness."

"Hadn't you better go into the house?" suggested Simon Potter, leading the way.

"Does any one know that she came here — any one but her mother?" asked the cashier, when they were seated.

"Yes; twenty girls know it; but it makes no difference," answered Prince. "You are to return to the city with Mollie, and take your place in the bank again, at once."

"You cannot mean that, Prince!" added Mr. Longimore, with a rather vacant expression.

"Don't keep him in suspense a single moment, Prince," pleaded Mollie.

"I will not. — The bonds were not burned, and they are safe in the bank vault at this moment, added Prince."

"Not burned! In the vault!"

"Precisely so, sir. I am sorry to say that my uncle is a bigger villain than I ever supposed him to be. To make a short story of it, though nothing is to be said about it in public just yet, uncle Fox must have taken the bonds from the bank on purpose."

"I have thought of that," interposed the cashier. "In my dungeon under the hay I could do nothing but think; and every incident of that eventful night has passed through my mind a hundred times. Why your uncle wished to show me, on that particular evening, where he kept his valuable papers, has often been a question with me. Mr. Bushwell has often been in the bank with me, after it was closed to the public, when he wished me to do some business for him. I had the impression very strong on my mind that I put the bonds back into the tin case. When I left him to get the blank checks he wanted, he must have changed the packages."

"The bonds were not burned. What you said to me the other night gave me an idea, which enabled me to look in the right place for them," added Prince, proceeding to tell the story of the hole in the chimney, in detail.

" I am sorry for your uncle. He set his house on fire to make it appear that the bonds were burned. How weak I was to flee, when, if I had remained, the truth might have been dis- covered earlier!"

" Perhaps not: we don't know," said Prince. " Uncle Fox, as it was, believed that no living being but himself knew anything about the bonds. If you had not left, and if people had not thought you were dead, he might have watched them better. But it's no use to talk about it now. Not a word is to be said to any one about the bonds."

" I shall not speak of them," replied the cash- ier; " though I shall be glad when the whole truth is known to everybody."

" Here is a letter for you, Mr. Longimore," added Prince, handing him the missive. " There is no bad news in it, or anything else that is bad."

With trembling hands the cashier tore open the envelope. The check dropped upon the floor as he did so, and Mollie picked it up.

"The directors are very kind to me; more so than I deserve," said the cashier, with tears in his eyes. "They invite me to return to my place without any delay. They have raised my salary, and made me a present of fifteen hundred dollars."

"We shall be happy again, father!" sobbed Mollie. "I knew you could not do anything wrong."

"But I have done wrong, my child. It was weak and cowardly for me to run away when the shadow of peril darkened my path; but I was beside myself; I lost my wits. The bonds were gone, and I was crazy."

"It is all right now, Mr. Longimore," interposed Prince. "We will not think any more about it. How did you get away without being seen by any one?"

"It was very early in the morning, and I saw no one stirring," replied the cashier. "I had no thought but of ending my life; and I took a boat at one of the wharves. I rowed out into the bay, intending to find rest from my anguish in a grave at the bottom of the deep waters of the bay. I thought only of my wife and children. I could not bear to think of going hence without a word to them. I wanted to tell them I was innocent of any crime. I felt that I could die in peace, if I could only tell them the truth. I pulled along the shore, and came to Simon Potter's house. He was the good Samaritan to me: he saved me."

The cashier grasped the hand of the strange man, who looked as solemn as an owl all the while, unwilling to admit, even by a smile, that he had anything like feeling in his composition.

"But where is the boat?" asked Prince.

"Tain't fur off. I took care on't," answered Simon Potter.

"I didn't mean to steal that boat, any more than I did the bonds," said the cashier.

"The boat's out of sight, under water; but she shall be returned in good order," added the recluse. I sunk her to keep her from tellin' any tales out o'school. I'll git her up at low tide to-day."

"Glad as I am to go home, Simon Potter, I don't like to leave you here," continued Mr. Longimore, taking the unwilling hand of his host again. "You have been more than a brother to me."

"No, I hain't. When folks turned agin you, and hunted you down, and every man's finger was turned onto you, I had a feller-feelin' for you. Besides you never laughed at me.

"I don't like to leave you here alone, Simon Potter. Make my house your home. You shall be cherished and cared for in sickness and health," continued Mr. Longimore.

"No; I shall stay here's long's as I stay anywhere. I don't want to see nobody nor nothin', unless it's a feller critter cast out and trod under foot of other men. Then I'm willin' to do sumthin' fur him. Good by, Mr. Longimore,"

Simon Potter shook hands with the cashier; but when Mollie, expressing her thanks, attempted to do so, he dodged her; and the little party withdrew.

"He has a good heart, and it's a pity he should be so odd," said the cashier, as they walked down to the mouth of the river. "But I suppose he is happier here all alone than he would be any where else."

On the shore, Prince hailed the fleet, and, in a single line, the boats came into the cove, bringing their stems up to the flat rock.

"Why, Mr. Longimore!" exclaimed Minnie Darling, who was the first to recognize him.

"Mr. Longimore!" cried a dozen others.

"He is your passenger, Minnie; for he will wish to go in the boat with Mollie," said Prince.

"But where has he been?" demanded Nellie. "We thought he was dead."

"He has been down here for a few days, taking the country air," laughed Prince. "He is not dead, and he will return to the bank at once. I want to assure you that all the directors believe him to be an honest upright and true man — as everybody will believe, when the whole truth comes out. Back out, Dorcas, and come about. Mollie, you can give the signals."

Mr. Longimore was already seated in the Dorcas, and she was hauled out from the shore. Mollie gave the orders, which set the rowers at work, very much to the astonishment of her father.

"I will take a seat in the Undine, if you please," said Prince.

"You are welcome, Professor Willingood," replied Susie Thaxter.

In a few moments all the boats were in line, the Dorcas leading the way. The rowing was simply beautiful, the movements of the fair rowists being grace itself. Presently Mollie elevated the signal, and with two motions to the left, brought the boats into pairs; and the order was kept in the most perfect manner. Again the signal "by fours" was given, and the four boats moved on abreast of each other. People ran to the shore to look at the pretty sight; and the praise bestowed upon the fair rowists was as hearty as it was general.

As the fleet approached the landing place, the signal "by twos" was given, and then "in single line." One by one the boats came in, and the members of the club all went on shore.

Attended by Mollie and Prince, Mr. Longimore hastened to his house, where the cashier pressed his wife and little ones to his heart, the great tears all the while streaming down his farrowed cheeks. From his house he went to the bank, where he was cordially greeted by all the directors, who had been waiting his arrival. The bonds were in the vault, and he was treated more like a general returning in triumph from

the conquest, than one who had fled in dismay
and terror from his post of duty. He told his
story over again, but it did not vary from that
related by Prince. He drew the check presented
to him by the directors; and when told what
the Dorcas Society had done for his family, he
hastened to return the two hundred dollars,
loaned to his wife, to Nellie Patterdale, the
treasurer. The result of this payment was, that
Don John at once received an order to build
another boat for the Dorcas Club, so that all
our girls could be afloat at the same time.

Mr. Longimore paid the note he had given
Fox Bushwell, a few days later, and Prince
returned him the bill of sale. Simon Potter
sent the boat in which the cashier had escaped
back to the city, to the great satisfaction of the
owner.

CHAPTER XVIII.

THE TRUTH WILL COME OUT.

ON the day Mr. Longimore returned from
his exile in the Northport woods, Fox
Bushwell went to a town twelve miles from the
city, to look after a delinquent debtor, who had
failed to pay his interest. He carried the note
and mortgage in his pocket, intending to take
possession of the property if the money was not
paid. The debtor had promised to pay the interest in the city when it was due; and it was
now a week after the time. Fox Bushwell was
an earnest advocate of the pleasures and bene-
fits of pedestrianism. No livery stable keeper,
no hack driver, no stage proprietor could draw
a dollar from his pocket for a ride — walking
was more healthy and agreeable. It was delightful, in the spring time, to tramp over the
country roads, inhaling the freshness of the pure

air, and gazing upon the beauties of Nature. It cost nothing.

The money-lender went on foot to the town twelve miles distant, and found his debtor sick abed; but he had the money in the house to pay his interest, and he paid it. The creditor made nothing by his journey but his dinner. The debtor would have sent his son to drive him back to the city, but the horse was lame.

Fox Bushwell was very tired when he reached his destination, and in no condition to expatiate upon the delights of pedestrianism, especially in its application to an elderly man who starved himself on herring, salt fish, and baked beans. He rested till the middle of the afternoon, and then walked home. Twenty-four miles in one day was too much for him; and, besides the weariness of the delightful tramp, he had taken a severe cold, by overheating himself, and then sitting down in a cold, damp place by the roadside. He was utterly exhausted when he reached his house, late in the evening. In the night he was sick, and Mrs. Pining was kept up half the night with him. Prince wanted to call in a doctor; but this was a piece of extravagance to which the money-lender would not submit.

"Doctors don't do no good in this sufferin',
dyin' world, and cost heaps of money," moaned
the widow. "I guess I can git him into a
sweat, and then he'll feel better."

Mrs. Pining did succeed in starting a perspiration on the shrivelled skin of her patient, and
he went to sleep. In the morning he was better, but in a very feeble condition. The insurance business was to be settled that day; and
when the old man spoke of going to the office
of the company, the housekeeper protested.

"Sufferin' you be, and dyin' you want to be,
if you think of goin' out arter such a sweat as
I gin you last night," said Mrs. Pining.

"I don't feel able to go, but I must. I want
to git that insurance, so I can pay you," whined
the money-lender.

The widow thought it was quite proper to
get the insurance, and pay her; so, having protested in due form, she offered no further oppo-
sition to the will of her employer. Fox Bushwell went to the insurance office; he walked
with a slow step and painful, leaning heavily on
his cane. When he arrived at his destination
he was very much astonished to see so many

people in the room, for his late return *from* his
pedestrian tour had prevented him from hearing any of the current news of the day. Nobody ever went to the miser's house except on
business; and even Mrs. Pining had not heard
of the return of the cashier. Though Prince
knew all about it, he did not care to tell the
news at home; and thus it fell out that Fox
Bushwell, in giving himself up to the enjoyment
of his long walk, with the pure air and the
beauties of Nature, failed to be in possession of
a piece of intelligence which might have changed
his whole course of action. In a word, he did
not know that Mr. Longimore had come back
and resumed his place in the bank; if he had
known it, doubtless his answers to the questions
put to him by Mr. Doane would have been entirely different, and, possibly, utterly inconsistent
with what he had before declared to be the
truth.

"I am sick this morning, Mr. Doane," moaned
the money-lender, as he entered the well-filled
room. "I had a bad turn last night, and I'm
not fit to be here to-day. It is high time that
insurance money was paid."

"Take a chair, Mr. Bushwell. I have no doubt we shall be able to settle the matter in some way, this time," replied Mr. Doane.

"I suppose you mean to pay me the money — don't you? I can't afford to lose it. I'm a poor man, and the loss comes hard on me."

"I wish to ask you some questions, Mr. Bushwell," added the president of the bank, who held the same office in the insurance company.

"I think you have asked me about questions enough," groaned Fox Bushwell.

"It does not look like a clear case yet," continued Mr. Doane. "Did you see Mr. Longimore on the evening before your house was burned?"

"I did. I told you that before. I've said so twenty times," answered the money-lender, petulantly. "I lent him some money, and — "

"Very well," interposed the president. "After you had finished the business connected with the loan, what occurred that evening?"

"Nothing, that I know of."

"Did Mr. Longimore leave your house as soon as the papers were signed and witnessed?"

"Why yes; of course he did. He didn't stay there all night," whined the miser.

" Did you go down cellar after the business was finished ? "

" I did. I've said so twenty times."

" Did Mr. Longimore go down cellar with you ? "

Fox Bushwell was startled, and the cold sweat stood on his forehead. It might have been weakness; it might have been something else. Why did Mr. Doane ask that question, which he had not put before?

" Did Mr. Longimore go down cellar with me ? " he repeated.

" That's the question I asked. Will you be kind enough to answer it ? "

" What should he go down cellar with me for ? "

" That does not answer my question."

" Of course he didn't go down cellar with me," replied Fox Bushwell, desperately.

" He did not ? "

" I say he did not. What business — "

" Never mind the reasons, Mr. Bushwell. All we want is the facts. Mr. Longimore did not go into the cellar with you ? "

" No, he did not. You talk to me just as if

23

you thought I was lying. Let me remind you
that I'm a clergyman."

Fox Bushwell tried to stand upon his dignity; but just then he had none to stand
upon.

"Where did you keep your valuable papers
when you lived in the house that was burned,
Mr. Bushwell?" asked the president.

"In my secretary most of them," replied the
old man, wondering why that question was
asked.

"Did you keep any of them in your cellar?"
said Mr. Doane, sharply.

"Well, yes; I kept some of them in the cellar," stammered the money-lender.

"In a brass kettle, hidden in the wall—did
you not?"

"Some of them," gasped Fox Bushwell; and
it was plain enough to him, by this time, that
somebody had been prying into his affairs.

"Did you show Mr. Longimore where you
kept the papers?"

"No, I didn't. I didn't show anybody where
I kept them."

"Very well, Mr. Bushwell: that will do on

that point," added the president. "What time
did you go to bed on the night of the fire?"

"About half past ten, as I told you."

"Wasn't it later than that?"

"No; I don't think it was."

"Wasn't it twelve?"

"No; nor eleven."

"Very well, Mr. Bushwell. Now, when you
saw Mr. Longimore that morning after the fire,
did he say anything about the bonds that were
lost?"

"What has that to do with my insurance?"

"I think a connection between the fire and
the bonds can be shown. I will thank you to
answer the question."

"I've told you twenty times what passed
between Mr. Longimore and me. I haven't
anything different to say. I'm a clergyman, and
I think what I say ought to be believed,"
moaned the money-lender.

"Do you say that Mr. Longimore did not
mention the bonds to you?"

"I do say so."

"I hope you will consider the matter well,
Mr. Bushwell," added the president. "You

may be called upon to testify in court on this subject."

"I'm a clergyman, and my word ought to be as good as my oath."

"It ought to be; but it is not. I know you were a clergyman once; but you are not an honor to the cloth; and it was well for the profession that you left it," said Mr. Doane, severely.

"I'm a poor sick man and I don't think it's right for you to insult me."

"Though you do not speak the truth, Mr. Bushwell, I purpose to do so. The insurance company will formally refuse to pay your claim for loss."

"Refuse to pay!" gasped Fox Bushwell; and to him this was certainly "the most unkindest cut of all." "I didn't think that of you. I paid the premium, and now you want to cheat me out of my money."

"You cheated yourself out of it," replied Mr. Doane.

"I'm a poor man, and I can't afford to bear this loss." groaned Fox Bushwell, rising slowly from his arm-chair, under the excitement of the unexpected decision against him.

"Mr. Bushwell, the directors are satisfied that you set your house on fire yourself."

"I! Why, Mr. Doane! How could you think such a thing of me — of me, a clergyman?"

"I will state the facts to you, as we understand them; and then, if you wish for the evidence, you shall have it," continued the president. "After Mr. Longimore had given you your package of private papers in the bank, you exchanged it for the bundle of bonds. In the cellar of your house, you took pains to show the cashier where you kept your valuable papers, and placed the package, which he supposed to be your own papers, — but which you knew to be the bonds, — in that brass kettle. After the fire, you visited the cellar, and satisfied him that your papers had all been burned. Very early in the morning the cashier found your private papers in the bank, and it appeared to him then that the bonds had been destroyed, instead of the bundle belonging to you. He went to you, and demanded the bonds at daylight; and you satisfied him that they had been burned. In an agony of grief and terror, Mr. Longimore fled. This is the truth."

"Not one word of it is ture!" cried Fox Bushwell, trembling in every fibre of his frame. "I haven't seen the bonds. I don't know anything about them."

"You want the proof, and you shall have it," replied Mr. Doane. "Send for Mr. Longimore!"

"Mr. Longimore!" gasped the money-lender, sinking back into his chair.

But he realized that he was losing his own case by his emotion, and he struggled to recover his self-possession.

"The cashier stole the bonds! He has made up this story to clear himself," groaned the wretch.

Fox Bushwell was utterly confounded, for the moment, when he saw the cashier enter the room. Mr. Longimore told his story precisely as the president had related it.

"He stole the bonds himself!" howled the money-lender. "He owes me money, and he wants to ruin me. Didn't he run away? Don't that prove it? Will you take his word against a clergyman's?"

"Mr. Bushwell, if you put the bonds into

that brass kettle in your cellar, we are under
obligations to you for removing them before you
set the house on fire," continued the president.
" By this act of forethought on your part they
were saved from the fire. Here they are."

Mr. Doane tossed the package on the long
table in front of the money-lender. If Fox
Bushwell was confounded before, he was overwhelmed now. He was a pitiable spectacle as
he reclined in the arm-chair, shaking like one
affected with palsy, and groaning like one in
the agonies of a violent distemper. His malady
was Sin, finding him out; but it was aggravated
by the illness under which he was suffering. No
one spoke for a long time; and after a while
the sufferer recovered in a measure.

" This bundle of bonds was found in the house
where you are living now, concealed in the arch,
under the chimney, where you had walled them
into the brick-work. This fact completes the
evidence. It is all that is necessary to prove
the case, though more can be produced," said
the president.

Fox Bushwell fainted away then, exhausted
by the excitement in his feeble condition. He

did not ask who had found the bonds, and the president was considerate enough not to mention the name of Prince. The money-lender realized that the evidence was complete. There was nothing on which he could hang a single hope ; and with the conviction of the truth came the loss of his senses. Dr. Darling, who was one of the directors, hastened to his assistance ; and when he was partially restored he was conveyed in a carriage to his home.

"Sufferin', dyin' world!" groaned Mrs. Pining, when the old man was brought into the house. "I knowed jest how 'twould be! I warned him ; but he wouldn't hear to nothin' I said. We are all lost creeturs!"

Prince assisted at the bedside of his uncle, and did all he could to assuage his moral and physical sufferings ; but the patient grew worse every hour. His sickness saved him from arrest as an incendiary the next day ; but Fox Bushwell was in the wild delirium of a fever, and knew nothing about the visit of the sheriff to his house. Dr. Darling came to him twice or three times every day. Prince and Mrs. Pining divided the days and nights between them, at his bedside.

"Mr. Longimore!" gasped the Money-lender.   Page 358.

In a week the end came, and the miser passed away, bereft of his reason, and unable to take leave of the money-bags for which he had sold his manhood, his honor, his own soul. Not many followed him to the grave, for he had no relatives, and his life had shut him out from the friendships of this world.

Prince was more shocked than grieved at the death of his uncle. His cheerless home was more gloomy than ever, for the memory of evil deeds seemed to hang heavy about it. On the evening after the funeral he called upon the Longimores. They did not attempt to console him, but they spoke not unkindly of the dead.

"This event will make a great change in your way of life, Prince," said the cashier. "At your age, you can nominate your own guardian, and if he is a proper person, the court will appoint him. I was thinking of the matter, and I was going to suggest the name of—"

"I am much obliged to you for thinking of me, Mr. Longimore," interposed Prince; "but I have my mind about made up."

"O, you have! Well, of course I don't

wish to influence you; but I was going to mention the name of Mr. Doane," added Mr. Longimore.

"I should like to live in the family of my guardian, if he suits me; and Mr. Doane is a rich man; he would not want me as a boarder."

"You can board where you please."

"If I can, I should prefer to board with you; and, to make the matter easier, I intend to name you as my guardian."

"Indeed! I'm sure I never thought of that," replied Mr. Longimore. "I owe my very life and reputation to you, Prince, as well as the happiness of my family; and I assure you I shall do all I can to serve you. I only desire that you may grow up a true and useful man, that your aims and impulses may always be as high as they are now."

Nothing more was said about the matter at that time; but at the next session of the Probate Court, the cashier was nominated and appointed the guardian of Prince. He was afterwards appointed administrator of the estate of Fox Bushwell, of which the nephew was the sole heir, so that it was not necessary to separate the two estates, which it was found, would have been a very difficult job.

To the great astonishment of the cashier, he found that he had the care of about a hundred thousand dollars all of which was invested at high rates of interest.

"Prince you can afford to live at the best hotel in the city; and I should feel justified in paying your board there," said the guardian.

"If you will let me board in your family, I shall be better satisfied," replied the ward.

"I shall be very glad to have you in my family."

This matter was settled, and the young man was provided with a nice room. The liberality of his new guardian enabled him to stock it with all the books he wanted; and Prince was happier than he would have been at a first-class hotel. Mollie Longimore went back to the High School; and those pleasant walks to and from the temple of learning were resumed, apparently as much to the satisfaction of the one as the other.

Mrs. Pining staid at Fox Bushwell's house till all these arrangements had been completed;

then the house was let and the furniture sold. The old lady had been very much troubled by her relations to the estate of her late employer.

"I hain't got no note nor nothin' in this sufferin', dyin' world, to show that Fox Bushwell owed me a cent!" said she, on the day after the administrator was appointed.

"You shall be paid, with interest, Mrs. Pining, if I have to pay you myself after I am of age," replied Prince. But I am sure Mr. Longimore will do everything that is right."

"It's no more'n right. I hain't had no interest for two years; and Mr. Bushwell owed me forty-eight dollars."

"Did he pay your wages, Mrs. Pining?" asked Prince.

"Goodness knows he didn't do nothin' o' the sort. Sufferin', dyin'! I guess not! I never had nothin' but my board."

"If I were you, I should present a bill for wages."

"Wages!" exclaimed the bewildered relic. "Mr. Bushwell never paid me no wages."

"He ought to have done so; and his administrator can do so now. The money will come out of me in the end, as I am the heir; but I shall not object."

"Wal, now, I declare!" gasped the widow. "How fur back can I go?"

"Six years. I don't think the administrator can pay for a longer time."

"That's long enough. I never was so struck up in my life. Sufferin', dyin'! Six years! How many weeks are they in that time, Prince? You're better'n I am at figgers."

"Three hundred and twelve."

"Airthquakes and applesass! If I charge two dollars a week will it be too much?"

"No, not at all."

"How much will that make, Prince?"

"Six hundred and twenty-four dollars."

"We're all sufferin' creeturs; and I never knowed there was so much money in the world! Mr. Longimore never'll pay no such wages."

"I think he will. Make out the bill, and we will try it, at any rate."

"Sufferin', dyin'! I ain't much at readin' and writin'."

"I will do it for you."

"You're a good boy, arter all, Prince" added

Mrs. Pining, almost overwhelmed by this sudden expectation of wealth.

She did not say that her wages had been the hope that Fox Bushwell would make her his wife, and thus insure her a home to the end of her days. Prince thought it no more than justice that she should be paid for her service, whatever the bargain with her employer had been. She received the full amount which Prince suggested, and the principal and interest of the debt. She found another place as housekeeper; but miserly and half-witted as she was, she was filled with gratitude to Prince, though she feared that the miser would rise from his grave to reproach her for taking wages for her labor.

Three weeks later, Don John completed the Fairy, — the fifth boat belonging to the Dorcas Club, — and it was a happy day, when for the first time all " our girls " were afloat at the same time. For this occasion a picnic down the bay had been arranged, and as the day proved to be mild and pleasant, the excursion was extended over to Turtle Head, where the fleet of the Yacht Club was at anchor.

As the little squadron approached Turtle Head,

two guns were fired by Commodore Montague's sloop, and all the yachtmen cheered till they were hoarse. A collation was served to the fair rowers, and everybody seemed to be at the high-water of rejoicing. In the afternoon, the first race of the season was organized, for the girls were by this time competent to pull a rapid stroke without injury. Prince would not permit the race to extend beyond half a mile.

" One — two — three — go! " shouted Prince, and every boat started at the same instant.

For some time they seemed to be rowing " by fives; " but pretty soon the Dorcas began to forge ahead, — perhaps because the girls in it were older and stronger. She held this advantage to the end, and came in ahead. The Undine was second, the Psyche third, the Lily fourth, and the Fairy last. Then Commodore Montague declared that it was a shame no prizes had been provided, and in a gallant speech he presented the leader of the winning boat a bouquet of sea-weeds, which made a deal of fun.

During the season, these excursions were often repeated, and the enjoyment of them was all but supreme. The *physique* of the girls was greatly improved, and they were all as brown and ruddy as the daughters of the farmers. But our story will be finished when we have said that Prince was very happy in the family of the Longimores, and that they — especially Mollie were equally happy in having him as a member of their circle. Probably the cashier will never be anything but a cashier; but he is in very great danger of having an excellent young man, worth about one hundred thousand dollars, for a son-in-law, — for Prince and Mollie, as they grow older, seem to be of the same mind.

Simon Potter was found dead in his lonely cottage one day, by a peddler who called to sell him some tin ware. Among his papers was found a will, which made Mr. Longimore and his heirs his sole legatees. The estate yielded only four thousand dollars, but the cashier paid off the mortgage on his house with it, and was happy to "owe no man anything."

The Dorcas Society continued to do its good work among the poor of the city, blessing hundreds by its labors and its charities, while the members continued, season after season, to win health and strength from the recreations of THE DORCAS CLUB.